MW01385982

HANDS-ON MARKETING

The Small Business Owner's Guide
to Advertising and Branding

DARIA MALIN

Boost Strategic Coaching
boostcoaching.ca

ISBN 978-1-988172-22-4 (print)
ISBN 978-1-988172-23-1 (ebook)

Cover Design: David Molesky of Rock & Bloom
Advertising Toolbox Graphic: Rock & Bloom

Published by Norseman Books
www.NorsemenBooks.com

TABLE OF CONTENTS

FOREWORD

WHAT TO EXPECT FROM THIS BOOK

Since the time I started studying marketing at university, I have found that most of the resources available on the subject of advertising seemed to be either written for big brand advertising and national companies, or about general concepts and ideas rather than concrete "how-to" guides for small independent business owners. More recently, it seems that any ebook, LinkedIn article, or blog post on the subject only teaches online marketing. They leave out or minimize the important role that mass media plays in successfully advertising and branding businesses, especially small ones.

This book is designed to help you understand all the facets of the advertising world and all the most common tools available to you as a small business. We'll cover what to say to your customers and how you should say it to make the biggest impact. We'll also study a group of small but mighty advertisers I've worked with over the past fifteen years. We'll see how they've applied these tools and find out why they have been so successful.

In true workbook form, you'll find "homework" at the end of each chapter. These will be questions and activities designed to help you apply the ideas in this book to your own business and think about advertising from an entirely new perspective. At the end of the book, I'll walk you through the process of putting together your own advertising

Action Plan. You can also access a PDF workbook at www. boostcoaching.ca/hands-on.

WHO IS THIS BOOK FOR?

When it comes to advertising, it's clear that mega-corporations have the budget to hire entire marketing departments to take care of the details. There are tons of ad agencies out there that run huge national and international campaigns for companies with massive marketing and advertising budgets. But that's not you.

As a small business owner, you have to be everything—CEO, store manager, HR, and of course the marketing department. The responsibility is all on you to become a jack of all trades and master every single part of your business. Since you're in charge, you know you can't just throw money at something and hope it works. Every dollar you put into your company must have a positive return, but the world of advertising seems overwhelming and expensive.

Should you focus on social media marketing like everyone says you should? What about billboards or radio ads? Are you ready to go all-in on a TV ad? Sure, you could keep trying out different options, but you don't want to spend the money if you don't really know if it will work, and that is completely reasonable.

That's why I've put this guide together for you. No more guesswork. No more wasted dollars with no return. This guide is specifically for owner-operated small businesses that want and need to advertise, but just don't know where to start. We'll cover the basics of branding and developing a message, and then get into the nitty-gritty of all your advertising options. By the time you're finished with this book, you'll have an advertising Action Plan customized to your specific needs. No more wondering which advertising avenues are worth it, and no more wasting money and time on ads that don't bring in customers.

A BIT ABOUT ME

I have spent the last 20 years studying and working in the world of advertising. Like many people in advertising, I am afflicted with the curse of not being able to just watch television, waste time on Facebook, or go for a drive like a normal human. Instead, I notice radio commercials and billboards. I analyze and judge them. I can't shop like a normal customer because I get caught up studying the sales process, customer experience, and merchandising.

I've interviewed literally hundreds of small business owners over the years as their media rep. Seeing the effects of their good and bad decisions has taught me a lot about what it takes to be successful in advertising. All too often, confused business owners tell me that when it comes to their advertising they "throw a bunch of stuff at the wall and see what sticks." When every media rep has the "best" product or promotion to sell, and each option is presented in a fancy package by an enthusiastic person who means well, how do you decide where to commit your limited, hard-earned marketing dollars?

After 20 years in advertising, I opened my consultancy where I work with clients on the concepts you'll find in this book. The focus of my coaching and the intention of this book is to provide clarity and direction for business owners as they develop a solid marketing plan and carry it out successfully. Although we're focusing primarily on advertising in this book, I work with my clients on all areas of business development including sales, customer service, and networking, so you will find a few tips and tricks on those areas as well.

With this book I aim to help you get the most out of your marketing budget and show you how to navigate the complex world of small business advertising. So, let's get started on bringing clarity and simplicity to your advertising.

INTRODUCTION

AN EXTREMELY BRIEF HISTORY OF ADVERTISING

For almost as long as humans have walked the earth, advertising has been a part of our world. Wall and rock paintings for commercial advertising can be traced back to 4000 BC. Papyrus was used for sales messages and wall posters by the ancient Egyptians. Shop owners sought the attention of customers with store signs showing images of shoes, groceries, and hats. Street callers invited passersby to purchase fruits and vegetables off the backs of carts.

With the invention of the printing press in the 1400s, communications throughout the world changed. Not only did the printing press pave the way for newspapers and mass publishing, but it introduced pamphlets, flyers, and posters to the world. Printed advertising could finally be produced in large numbers, so businesses took advantage of the opportunity to reach a wider customer base.

By the 19th century, advances in technology brought print advertising to newspapers, leading to the first opportunity for nationally recognized brand names to emerge. By the early 20th century we had global ad agencies and a $3 billion advertising market in the United States. Radio in the 1920s and television in the 1950s both revolutionized the advertising industry and ad campaigns started to influence, and even become a part of, pop culture.

With the advent of the Internet, online marketing has created an entirely new way to reach even more people. With every advance in technology, the world of advertising grows in size and complexity.

Advertising today

This just in: all big screen billboard advertising in New York's Times Square has been removed. The word on the street is that traditional advertising is dead, so city officials have announced the removal of all advertising from the area, stating, "We assume that visitors must be looking down at their mobile phones and not seeing the billboards anyway."

Ok, obviously I made that up. But doesn't it seem like that is where the world is headed? Everything you read about marketing these days shouts, "Traditional advertising is dead! Online advertising and social media marketing are the only things that will save you and reach your customers!" And you're being told you need to focus all your efforts on building a social relationship with each one of your customers—not advertise to them.

So, why is it that billions of dollars are still being spent on billboards, network TV ads, and radio? Why do you get a mailbox full of flyers every week? According to PwC's Outlook Report, in 2016, businesses spent $136 billion on "traditional" advertising vehicles (TV, radio, print, and out-of-home) in the US, and the industry is only growing. Are all the big brands getting duped into spending their advertising budgets in these dying media, year after year? Should we break it to all those who are buying up the flashy screens in Times Square that they are wasting their money and reaching nobody? Or, should we be asking, "What is it that they know that you and these marketing columnists don't?"

In the third quarter of Super Bowl XLVII in New Orleans, Baltimore had a 28-6 lead over the San Francisco 49ers. The game came to a halt when a power outage cut the lights in the Superdome for 34 minutes and earned the game the nickname The Blackout Bowl. During the blackout, somebody on the marketing team for Oreo Cookies tweeted, "Power out? No Problem." The post was linked to a picture of an Oreo cookie, with a caption that said, "You can still dunk in the dark." Oreo had a smart idea and turned it around in a matter of minutes.

In that same game, Budweiser ran a TV commercial about Budweiser Clydesdales featuring a horse who was reunited with his trainer. It was a touching story told using movement, music, and emotion.

The Wall Street Journal, Marketing Week and all the other major marketing communities from the US to Great Britain and Australia were raving about the Oreo tweet, claiming that it owned the Super Bowl. It's true; the Oreo tweet was a great idea. It gained media attention and reached a wide audience. But was it really as successful as they say it was?

Think about these statistics: 64,000 people saw the tweet, even though 40 million people buy Oreos. Compare that to the 50 million people who saw Budweiser's 60-second TV ad. Although the Ravens won the game, the final score was 64,000 for Oreo (social media) to 50 million for Budweiser (traditional media). Yet all attention and credit was given to Oreo.

If you search online, you'll find article after article with titles like "Traditional advertising is dead" and "Let's just call traditional media dead and move on with our lives." In business writing, it is acceptable to make claims like this without any data to back them up. And without anyone contradicting the claims, many marketers take them as fact.

Does something feel off to you? Have you shifted the focus of your advertising to online media because of these headlines and wondered why you're not getting the results you were expecting? Do you have a feeling that marketing shouldn't be this complicated? If big corporations are still investing in traditional advertising and seeing results, why are marketing journalists claiming traditional advertising is dead?

If you've completely switched gears and moved all your eggs into the "online basket," but you're not getting the results you were expecting, you are not alone. You are probably finding it hard to keep up with all the moving parts of your online activities as the playing field keeps changing. Marketing your business and your brand should not be this complicated.

Let me be clear, my intention is not to attack online marketing. There are amazing tools available to you online and they can do fantastic things for your business. However, the business development work you can do from behind your computer desk is only part of the picture. To be successful, you, as a local business owner, need to be armed with the advertising tools that will have the biggest impact on your bottom line, including both online and traditional advertising.

But just like you don't need to use every possible social media outlet, you can pick and choose which traditional advertising avenues will work best for you and your audience. The point is definitely not to do everything, but to do the things that will bring in the biggest return on your investment. Let me guide you through the options and show you how to use these marketing vehicles to grow your business.

CHAPTER 1

Branding

"A brand is a reason to choose."

— Cheryl Burgess

The ultimate goal of marketing is to ensure that your business is the one that your customers think of *first* and feel the *best* about when they need what you sell. This is what we call *branding*, and it means you will have more people coming through your doors and more dollars coming into your till. You have successfully branded your business when your name is a red-hot cattle brand burned onto the memory of one individual customer and when your potential customers feel the way you want them to feel about your company; when they know exactly how your company can serve them.

Everyone from Google to your local t-shirt printer to the guy who will take care of your social media is offering to help brand your business. Most of them focus on your name, logo, tagline, colors, and the fancy pens you ordered with your phone number on them. But these features only help build your brand when meaning is attached. While they are all important brand elements, they are not the entirety of branding all by themselves.

Most marketers think that choosing teal and yellow for their company colors and using them on their logo, billboards, and décor is branding because they believe people will associate those colors with their company, notice their consistency, and remember them because of it. The truth is that branding is more than that. It is the story you are telling through your messaging and the customer experience that backs it up. These are what make people attach meaning to your logo and fancy pens when they see them. **Essentially, your brand is what is being said about your business when you are not in the room.** Before you spend time choosing your colors and logo, you need to know what meaning you want people to associate with your business. What do you want people to think of when they see your brand? How does it look, sound, smell, and feel?

IF YOU BUILD IT, THEY WILL COME...?

I always say that opening a business is like preparing for a party (though business owners will argue that it feels nothing like a party). You start your planning by choosing a theme, then you create and put up decorations, yell at your kids as you all scramble to clean the house, prepare and put out appetizers, stop at the liquor store to stock the bar fridge, go back out because you forgot ice, wipe your kids' faces and brush their hair, yell to go and clean up their toys (again), and then scramble to look like you're relaxed and in control when your guests arrive. Then you wait. And wait.

As the hours pass and no one shows up, it dawns on you: in all the chaos to get the party together, you forgot to send out the invitations! It looks like it's going to be a party just for you, because nobody else knows that there is anything even happening.

This is what happens when a business opens its doors and doesn't budget for advertising in the first year. I've seen it happen. Advertising is the first thing to get cut when it really should be a top priority. You need to get customers in the door to start generating sales.

I called on the owner of a small downtown giftware store a number of years ago. When I walked into her store for the first time, I was struck by how cozy it was and how nice it smelled. The lighting was beautiful and she had her merchandising set up perfectly. Everything inside that store was flawless, but something was fundamentally missing: customers! In all her planning and research, she had not allocated any resources to advertising or marketing the store. She thought, "If I build it they will come," and failed to send out an invitation to the community.

By the time we met, she had no money left to put toward advertising. Although it was one of the most beautifully decorated parties I've seen, I don't think the store lasted a year. An almost identical store opened around the same time as hers in an area of the city with a similar amount of drive-by traffic. The second owner focused on marketing her business consistently and has since won numerous awards and just celebrated her 10th anniversary in business. There was room for both stores, but only one had a voice in the market.

This is not a standalone case. Over my years as a media rep, I had hundreds of conversations with business startups. Whenever I met someone with that "if you build it they will come" attitude, I knew I'd more than likely see their closing-out sale within two years.

The reality is that having something great to offer is not enough. You also have to *communicate* that offer to your community—otherwise, no one will even know it's available to them. And that communication starts with having a story to tell.

You get to control the story

Whether you advertise or not, the market will have conversations about your business. All good businesses will grow by word of mouth, so the role advertising plays is that it allows you to *control* your brand and influence what people say about you. It serves as a really big mouth, reaching people faster and further than word of mouth can. If you don't advertise, the market will have conversations about you without your input. While that can be both good and bad, it takes the control out of your hands. By having a strong brand in place, you're insulated against the rare bad conversation by all the good things people hear, think, and say about your company.

Meet Brainsport. They are an independent shoe store that specializes in running shoes and apparel. They started their consistent advertising campaign after being in business for a number of years. In their first years of business without consistent advertising and branding, they allowed the market to create a story about them, rather than telling the story they wanted their customers to hear. Although the owner set out to serve not only avid runners, but also walkers, beginner runners, those who wanted to get into shape, and those who are on their feet all day at work, the story in the market was completely different.

When Brainsport opened, the market thought the store was for serious runners only. Those of us who like the idea of running, but slightly prefer sitting on the couch with a glass of wine and a Netflix series found it intimidating to walk into the store. It was easy for anyone who wasn't a serious runner to think, "This store is only for athletes. I don't know where to start with that huge wall of shoes. I will look like an idiot. This store isn't for me."

Brainsport succeeded in building a huge following of serious runners—you know, the kind that post their marathon photos on social media while the rest of us dislike them for being more motivated and in better shape—but was missing the rest of their target markets. With advertising, we set out to change the story by controlling the message through a consistent campaign that focused on the main benefit they offer: a pain-free day on your feet. And for a decade and a half, Brainsport has been speaking to not only avid runners, but grandparents, new moms, comic convention-goers, nurses, weekend warrior runners, and even Netflix and wine-loving wannabe athletes.

Brainsport succeeded in gaining new customers and reaching the markets they truly wanted because they took control of the story being told about them and started consistently telling people what they were about and who they were for. They changed how people perceive Brainsport and invited customers in to have their feet measured and matched to the right shoes. Brainsport has been successful because they learned to start controlling the message and they haven't stopped since.

Tribes

When companies do an especially outstanding job of building a good feeling associated with their brand and getting into the long-term memory of their ideal customer, they end up with a tribe following. Iconic examples are companies like Apple Computers and Harley Davidson Motorcycles. (I tried to make this the one business book that didn't refer to Apple in some way, but it seems to be impossible because they really have set the standard on how to do it right in so many areas of business.) They've built their tribes by selling more than just products: they sell their *why*.

In his book, *Start with Why: How Great Leaders Inspire Everyone to Take Action*, Simon Sinek explains that people don't buy *what* you do, they buy *why* you do it. The *why* is what makes the message stick or gets the company placed into long-term memory and associated with a good feeling.[1] Apple has been successful because they start with why they are in business: to challenge the status quo and "think different." All the products they create stem from this fundamental purpose. Their customers identify with that message and become disciples of Apple because their values match up. Apple makes them feel good about using their products because they feel like part of the Apple tribe and that fosters a sense of belonging.

Harley Davidson has gone beyond simply selling a product; they sell a lifestyle. Harleys are cool and tough so their owners are cool and tough. Their community of followers, Harley Owners Group (HOG), is passionate and loyal to this identity. HOGs represent and defend the brand because it has become a representation of who they are as people and they identify so closely with it that they basically do the marketing for Harley themselves. This community formed based on the personality and values of the brand when it first started because they knew *who they were* and who they wanted their customers to be. Since then, Harley Davidson has built themselves into an international identity. Anyone who identifies with this tribe and this lifestyle would never consider buying another brand of motorcycle.

Of course, Harley Davidson and Apple are international brands, so they have the market share and budgets to create these global tribes. When it comes to small businesses like yours, though, the concepts are the same, just on a smaller scale. When you brand yourself correctly, you start building your tribe in your local community. Take Brainsport as an example:

On a local scale, Brainsport has built a tribe. Their customers shop only at their store and run in the marathons they organize and sponsor. Brainsport hosts running clinics and weekly running clubs, which their tribe attends religiously. On top of that, the tribe supports and donates to Brainsport's charitable initiatives. In day-to-day life, Brainsport customers wear t-shirts, jackets, and socks with the Brainsport name and logo.

In their market, Brainsport represents fitness, an active lifestyle, getting outside, and building community. Their customers share these values and want to be part of that story. They have created a tribe based on the lifestyle their customers want to be associated with and many of these customers have become entirely loyal to them and their brand—and they don't hesitate to tell others about this excellent shop.

When you know who you are, what you do, and why you do it, and if you clearly communicate these things, eventually your tribe will find you. Your message and values (your branding) will determine who is attracted to your business and who will become fans, so you need to know who your target markets will be before you can start building and telling your story.

DECIDE WHO YOU WILL SERVE

You can't be everything to everybody, nor should you try to be. Instead, decide what you stand for and who you are going to serve. Don't worry about everybody else; there will be more than enough people looking for exactly what you have. As a business owner, there is the tendency to try to accommodate every type of customer, every price level, and every request. As soon as you blur your focus, though, the market gets confused about who you are and your brand gets muddled or forgotten.

Meet the Awl Shoppe—a store that's been in business for over 40 years. They sell luggage that will not fall apart when you travel, so you never have to worry about a broken handle, a ripped zipper, or a trail of clothes on the carousel at baggage claim. Whether you choose from their entry level or high end lines, you can rest assured you that you are buying quality merchandise.

It's great that they have this reputation, but it didn't happen by accident. As the business grew and reached more customers, the owners had to make some tough decisions. They chose to forget about the customers who can't afford expensive equipment in favor of focusing on stocking only high-quality products.

Over the years, they've been tempted to add a cheaper line so that anyone at any budget could shop there, but they knew it would hurt their brand. If they gave in and sold a cheap, low-quality set, their customers who purchased that particular set would end up disappointed and feeling as though they had been lied to. They chose to leave those budget shoppers to the big box stores and focus only on the people who would spend a little more to get a product that would last. As a result, the Awl Shoppe's story in the market matches their values; when you want the good stuff, you go to the Awl Shoppe.

WHAT IS YOUR MESSAGE?

When it comes to developing your own brand, you need to know who you are, why you're in business, and who you want to serve. *Before you even get into your merchandising or brand colors, go back to the basics.*

Once you know the who, what, and why of your business, you can start figuring out what your target market wants to hear. If you are a kids' clothing store, are you targeting busy budget shoppers or moms who only want the best? How would your message be different for each of these audiences?

For a budget shopper, you would probably focus on saving money and time. For a mom who only wants the best, you would focus on high-end, high-quality products and keeping up with trends. So, when developing your message and determining the story you want to tell, start with who you are and who you want to serve, then figure out what they need and want to hear. We'll look at this in more detail in Chapter 2.

WINNING THE HEART

When it comes to purchasing products, **people make decisions with their hearts and justify those decisions with their minds.** You might think this is counter-intuitive, but the truth is that no matter how much research people put into their purchases, they still tend to "go with their gut" and rationalize it later.

After years of hearing our children beg for a dog and my father-in-law reminding me, ad nauseam, that every little boy should have a dog, my husband and I finally took the plunge. We spent a year researching breeds online and talking to friends and family who have different kinds of dogs. We finally defined which breeds would fit best within our busy, bustling household. We knew smaller breeds that don't shed much and don't need a lot of exercise made the most sense for us.

Then, we were invited over to a coworker's house for a visit. When we stepped through the door, we were greeted by a big, beautiful brown and white dog—a German Shorthaired Pointer. In the first few minutes together, we completely fell in love. Though this breed didn't fit within the practical parameters we had set, we knew we just had to get one of our very own.

Just a few months later, we welcomed our beautiful new German Shorthaired Pointer puppy into our home and of course had to adjust a few things to make it work. She sheds and needs long walks twice a day. But since we made an emotional decision about her, we continue to rationalize and justify the decision. Sure, she sheds more, but it's not that bad because her hair is short. Yes, she needs a lot of exercise, but we all like going out in the dead of winter when it's well below freezing out… And despite the impracticalities of our dog, we are happy to have a large, high-energy, shedding dog in our family!

In the same vein, people *can* buy clothes at Walmart. In practical terms, they will keep you covered and warm, and they come at the right price. But the reason people will buy a $600 Dolce & Gabbana t-shirt isn't to keep them covered and warm; it's for the feelings and lifestyle associated with the brand. No, it's not a logical purchase; it's a totally emotional buy. While someone may rationalize their decision by saying it will last sixty times longer than the $10 one, they actually purchase because the brand that has been built around that t-shirt causes customers to make emotional decisions about what they're buying. Many people buy their clothes to make a statement or to show a certain status. They might share values and beliefs with others who buy luxury goods and fashions like Dolce & Gabbana and want to be part of the tribe that's associated with that brand.

When you are planning your advertising message, take into consideration how much emotion, compared to logic, will be involved in the decision to buy what you are selling. Most business owners miss the boat with their messaging when they focus on the company and the features they offer—the message should be about the customer and the benefits to them. Speaking right to what the customer desires is what makes people notice your message. This is what allows them to cut through the clutter and make your voice heard. It's like hearing the one person speaking English in a crowd of people who are speaking French.

Your customers are selfish

I don't mean that in a bad way—your customers rock and we love them. But the fact is we all have to be selfish to weed through the clutter around us. We can only focus on the things that make a difference in our world, so we block out the majority of the messaging we are hit with. As much as I'd like to tell you that your customers will support you simply because you are locally owned or because you're great people, that's just not always true. While your customers may prefer supporting locally owned businesses, it's probably because supporting local makes them feel good, which is a selfish benefit.

However, if your prices are double what Amazon charges and you provide no additional benefit, like better service, more expertise, or better quality, then you can't expect loyalty. Branding is all about the customer, so you need to know what they want and then give that to them. When developing your message and your brand, you always have to be asking, on behalf of your customer, "WIIFM (What's In It For Me) if I choose to do business with you?" Make sure that shines through in your messaging and you'll get them on board.

GET INTO THEIR LONG-TERM MEMORY

Most advice on advertising instructs you to figure out a way to be in front of your potential customer when they are most motivated to buy. Business owners struggle with this, not knowing how to predict when their customer will make that decision or where to place their message so they can make an impression at that particular moment.

But to effectively brand your business, you have to take the opposite approach. Rather than trying to predict when your customer will make a decision and being there when they choose to buy, branding strives to be there *before* the decision is made by building and maintaining awareness and finding your way into the long-term memory of your potential customers. You win the branding race when you have interested your customer and spoken to them enough that they can't help but think of you when they or someone they know needs you. If you wait until the moment they're ready to buy to try and convince them of your worth, you're too late.

Imagine a pipe breaks under your sink and there is water spraying everywhere. Do you look through your flyers and figure out which home improvement store will be the best option? Of course not! You just get in your car and drive straight to Home Depot because they communicated with you consistently for years before you needed to fix your sink.

Roy H. Williams is a best-selling author known for his *Wizard of Ads* trilogy. He has tens of thousands of readers for his *Monday Morning Memo* and is a marketing consultant and the founder of the Wizard Academy. Williams has spent years reading study after study on the neuroscience of information processing. He has taken his knowledge and expertise and applied it to his consulting, writing, and courses about the world of advertising.[2]

Regarding how branding works in our brains, Williams tells us, "Neurologically, branding occurs in long-term, involuntary procedural memory; the product of salience times repetition."[3] In other words, the weaker your message, the more repetition is required. A message that is interesting to the audience, repeated often enough, will be remembered and recalled when someone needs what you've been telling them you can provide.

So, the effectiveness of your advertising is dependent on two factors: how interesting your message is to your audience and how often you repeat that message to them.

SALIENCE AND REPETITION

In his book, *Secret Formulas of the Wizard of Ads*, Williams defines branding as getting customers to attach a feeling to your business. In other words, branding is planting an associative memory in the minds of your customers. Just like Pavlov's dog, every time your industry comes up, you want people to think of your company.

Ivan Pavlov conditioned his dog by giving him meat every time he rang a bell. Over time, the dog learned that when the bell rang, he should expect food, so he salivated. But it was only after Pavlov had done this many, many times, that the dog would salivate just from hearing the bell. The bell itself didn't matter to the dog, it was the taste of the meat that he wanted. Just like this, branding happens with repetition. You customer has to hear from you many times before they automatically associate you with your industry, and the message must be mouthwatering.

If you tell your audience something they care about in your messaging—something that is salient to them—only then will they be inclined to act when you ring the bell. Business owners often spend too much time talking about the features of their business (the bell) and not enough time on the benefits they offer customers (the meat). That's why a great deal of the messaging out there misses the boat.

ASSOCIATE A GOOD FEELING WITH YOUR BUSINESS

"I'd like to buy the world a Coke…"

Coca-Cola's brand vision is said to be the universal icon for happiness. From a hilltop in Italy in 1971, youth from all over the world sang, "I'd like to buy the world a Coke," spreading warm and fuzzies around the globe. We've sung, "Always Coca-Cola," and, during the 2010 World Cup, "When I get older, I will be stronger…just like a waving flag." The recent Share-a-Coke campaign inspired a feeling of camaraderie by encouraging people to share a Coke with a friend whose name was printed on the can. The campaign has led to a trend of sharing selfies with namesake cans on social media, resulting in a reported 998 million impressions on Twitter.

Even our modern-day image of a chubby, rosy-cheeked, jolly Santa Claus wearing red and white is said to have been made popular by the Coca-Cola Christmas ad series that started in the 1930s. Coca-Cola has taken a commodity product and, through their advertising and branding, created an association with happiness, excitement, pride, and nostalgia for generations.

You don't have to be on the global scale of Coca-Cola to make this work for you. Ask yourself what feeling you want associated with your business and how you can create that feeling in your immediate community.

Here are a few ideas:

BE REAL

You can build a good feeling about your company within your community by just being genuine, honest, and real. Your advertising can be clear on why you exist and send a warm invitation to your audience, letting them know you are there when they need you.

Telling your target market what they want to hear shouldn't be about providing false information and just "saying what they want to hear." Instead, it is about understanding what they want and need, providing that to them, and then communicating what you provide through your message and branding. The best way to do that is by being truly authentic and real with your customers. If you're a tiny mall with a handful of local businesses, tell that to your audience. Don't make your commercials sound like you're a high-fashion mall with brand-name retailers. That only leads to disappointment, which is nowhere close to the good feeling you are going for.

SUPPORT YOUR COMMUNITY

As a small business, becoming an integral part of the community can be a huge benefit to building your brand in a positive way. You could organize or sponsor local community events, raise funds for a specific charity, or volunteer your time to serve food at a local shelter. Business owners are asked for donations on a regular basis and usually cannot afford to say yes to everyone who asks, but you could set a monthly budget for cash or product donations or simply choose one or two causes to support and be consistent with them. It is okay to be strategic and slightly self-serving in your choices here, but your best benefit will come from a true desire to give back.

Starbucks, though they are now an international chain, started out by building good feelings for their brand in each community they moved into. Before there were stores on every corner and everyone knew their name, each time they opened a new location, Starbucks would hire a local PR firm to help them understand the heritage of that city and the causes the community supported. For each new market, they would plan at least one big community event to celebrate their arrival and then donate the proceeds to a local cause.[4] They have since followed through on the community event and sponsorship focus and this continues as part of their marketing, despite their international status.

Even though they are the "big guys," they are able to garner loyalty with locals and make a positive impact in each community. In fact, one of my business-owner friends lives and works in a very "buy local" neighborhood. He always chooses to meet me at Starbucks, even though there is a coffee shop right down the street that is locally owned and roasts their own beans on site. I asked him why he doesn't choose the local guys and he told me it's because, "They do nothing to support the community. They don't ever give donations to our kids' school, which is right across the street, or support any of the charity events we host." Starbucks always says yes, so that's what people remember about them.

BUILD A FEELING OF BELONGING

Meet Alex from Sardinia Family Restaurant. He has managed to create a little bit of magic at his unassuming Greek restaurant in a strip mall in the industrial part of town. Every day, he stands at the door welcoming people in to his "house." When talking about his customers, he says, "They're in my house, so I need to make sure they're taken care of. I will always find room in my house for them." His customers know him by name and he knows almost everyone who comes in frequently. When people eat at his restaurant, he is genuinely happy they have come to see him, doling out hugs and teasing the people he knows. He even goes around to every table to check if they're enjoying their meal or need a drink refill. Alex makes everyone feel welcome and like they belong, and lets them know he remembers them when they come back.

Here's a story that speaks volumes about his efforts: there was an older couple who came in every week for supper. He hadn't seen them in a while, so when he ran into the wife at the grocery store, he asked why she hadn't been in. She shared that her husband had passed away and she didn't want to go back to the restaurant because it felt like it had been "their" place. Alex was genuinely sad and told her, "You belong here. We want you to come back. You have to come back." When she did, he went out of his way to make her visit comfortable and enjoyable. His customers keep coming back because they feel like they belong. It's Alex's genuine effort to make everyone feel at home that has made Sardinia such a success.

This is something you can do in your own business. Not every place needs to feel like home, but when you know your customers (or your ideal customers), you can figure out what makes them most comfortable and feel as though they belong. This can come in many forms, like the way you design your store, the quality of the staff you hire, and how you personalize your communications with them. You can even go so far as to model Alex's behavior and welcome every new customer with open arms and care for them as individuals.

When you do that, people will never hesitate to visit, and will always associate your brand and your business to the great feeling they get when they need something from you. Not only will you stay top-of-mind, but they will want to spread the word about their excellent experience.

Solve a problem

Solving problems is key to running a successful business, not only because it attracts customers, but because it makes people feel good about you and your brand.

Meet Eb's Source for Adventure. They sell seasonal adventure equipment like kayaks, skis, and paddleboards. They have branded themselves not only as the place for adventure products, but as a place that has experienced staff who actually use the equipment they sell. The end benefit to the customer is that, with the right guidance and the right gear, they will have a better day in the snow or on the water. They have branded themselves well because they advertise who they are, and more importantly, why the audience should care. Ultimately, they are selling experiences and solving the problem of trying to enjoy a vacation while dealing with crappy equipment.

And the right equipment really does make all the difference. My husband and I used to go to an all-season resort up north to "get away from it all." (This was before we had kids, so I ask you, what did we think we were getting away from?!) We would rent a small cottage, do some skating or hiking, and relax by the fire in the evenings. During one trip, we rented cross-country skis to take out into the sparkly, snowy afternoon. My skis were circa 1975 and they were so terrible they didn't even slide smoothly over the snow. I had to push with all my might, and I actually keeled over halfway through the trail and told my husband to "please just leave me here to die." Thankfully, he didn't do that (in case you wanted to know) and instead helped me take off the skis so I could go back to the cabin to have hot chocolate while he finished the trail.

The next year, I decided to buy my own equipment before heading to the cabin. Since I knew I didn't want to waste a vacation using another set of terrible skis, I went to Eb's and appreciated their expertise and helpfulness. I left knowing they had solved my problem, and now I head to Eb's any time I need adventure equipment.

Eb's has been successful with their messaging because they have identified a problem: people don't have a good time when they have to fight with their equipment, like I did with the old skis. So, to create a better experience for customers and give themselves a leg up on their competitors, they hire experienced staff who can help you choose the right equipment for your needs. Then, when you leave the store, you feel great about your experience, and when you finally get out on the snow or water, you know Eb's was the right place to go. That's an experience customers remember.

KEEP IT SIMPLE

Business owners and marketing professionals alike have been guilty of overcomplicating the process of marketing. Your job as a marketer is to be as clear as possible with your message and as consistent as possible in the places you choose to advertise. If you are successful, those who need your service will identify themselves. The easier you make it for customers to understand what you do, the more likely they are to buy from you. If you make them work to figure it out, they're going to go somewhere else.

You don't have to be flashy or outside the box or even unexpected. You don't have to have a hundred moving parts. You just need to keep your message and your channels consistent and reach far enough that your customers can find out about you. Yes, sometimes gimmicks can pay off, and in some cases they are warranted, but in the long run, it's much better for your customer to know who you are and what you do than to be flashy. **Ask yourself this: are you trying to entertain your audience or persuade them?**

STAY CONSISTENT

A business stays branded in our minds like a lawn stays mowed. Unless you keep at it over time, your message and brand will disappear. This may seem overwhelming right now, but once you have your message decided, all you need to do is stay consistent with sending it out.

McDonald's, Coca-Cola, Apple and Walmart have all built their business on continuous, relentless messaging to the market. They didn't simply announce their opening and then rely on people to remember them for years to come. Even though everyone knows what McDonald's is, they continue branding because they still want be the first place you think of when you don't have time to make supper before your daughter's soccer game. McDonald's wants you to have that immediate recall and a positive association with them, so they didn't stop branding and marketing when they achieved worldwide awareness. No matter whether you're in New York, Paris, or Kiev, you'll see a McDonald's and think, "That's familiar to me and I know what I'm going to get there."

So what about you, the local small business? You're not likely to have international recognition or a global tribe following, but you can still build and maintain a consistent voice in the market. When you become the one who talks to the market most often, you'll get people in the door. Then, do a good job for them and they will keep coming back.

Think about an exceptional experience you've had at a restaurant in your city. You had the absolute best veggie burger you've ever tasted. The room was hopping, you ran into a bunch of people you know, and the wine gave you the perfect warm and fuzzy glow. When was the last time you were there? When someone asks you to pick a place to meet for dinner, do you always think of that place, or do you forget about it when the need arises? Then, when the name of the restaurant is mentioned do you say, "I love that place! I haven't been there in ages!"? If your business is silent in the market, those that are making more noise will get picked more often. **It's not your customer's job to remember you; it's your job to remind them.**

Anyone who has ever worked in sales knows that the real work starts after you've made the sale. Managing expectations, making sure the client is happy with their purchase, and keeping them happy long after they've left the store is where you will build brand loyalty and keep people coming back. Getting a customer to try you for the first time is the first goal, but keeping them engaged and coming back for the long-term is just as important.

How long does branding take?

You wouldn't believe how many small business owners say, "I tried advertising and it didn't work." And while it may not have worked in the short term, branding is a long-term commitment. I hate to break it to you, but just because you have announced your arrival, the world is not just going to drop what they're doing and rush to your doors. Most of your audience will be happy to know your business exists, but will they remember you when they need you? What about six months from now? Whether it's the flashing digital billboards we drive past downtown, the Coca-Cola poster on our neighbor's cubicle wall, or the radio ads playing over the speaker in the hair salon, there are so many messages hitting us every day, pushing your message from long ago right out of our minds.

How do you push through all of the advertising clutter to find that enviable place in our long-term memory? Consistency and repetition. Unless you're a greenhouse or a Christmas store, you are probably open for business 52 weeks of the year. Your message, then, should be sent out every one of those weeks for the entire life of your business. Think about a time where you heard about a great new restaurant opening in your city. You wanted to try it, but it took you three months before you could get there. If that restaurant only advertised for one month, they would have lost you as a customer, even if you had every intention of going. The key is to keep your message out there consistently so you stay top-of-mind for your customers.

A few years ago, when I worked as a media rep, a frozen dinner company starting advertising with me. They had a unique product line and very good food and the potential to become a huge hit. As we were setting up the advertising, I told them it would take a few months to build visibility before people would start including them in their purchase habits, especially since we were heading into the summer months. No matter how many times I reminded them that the first phase was laying the groundwork, they couldn't get past the fact that they weren't seeing very many new customers in those first few months of the campaign. Thinking they were being prudent, they decided to cancel their campaign at the three-month mark, right when that initial advertising would have started to pay off. They missed their opportunity to see the results of their marketing dollars because they were short-sighted in their goals.

Of course we all want to see immediate results, but that is simply not how branding and advertising usually work. McDonald's, Coca-Cola, Walmart, Harley Davidson, and Apple never stop actively branding. The principles that have made them world-class brands can make you a household name in your own community, but you have to have a long-term focus. Sure, you can advertise your opening for a few months, but that won't build you a brand.

RESULTS TAKE TIME

When you start advertising, you are first building visibility, then credibility, and finally profitability. It is essential to give your customers time to hear about you and pay attention to your message and then make the time to respond. That's why playing the long game is so important to advertising success. Although it's difficult when you don't see immediate results, you need to be patient.

We often called the first three to six months of a new ad campaign the "chickening-out period." This is the time when you are spending more on your campaign than it is making for you, and you are in the most danger of canceling your contract and ending your advertising efforts, just like that frozen dinner company. Chances are, if you chicken out in the first three to six months, you'll end up repeating the process with another advertising channel anyway, and you'll have to start from zero again.

The amount of work you'll need to put in to get to a point where your advertising will pay off greatly depends on the life cycle of the products you sell. If you're selling houses, it will take a lot longer to convert a prospect into a customer than if you are selling $10 lunches. We eat three or four times a day, so a restaurant's advertising will drive traffic more quickly because people can make the decision to go to a new place for lunch pretty much any day and you're asking for a very low investment.

When a home builder advertises, on the other hand, it obviously pays off in much larger increments, but over a longer period of time. Since people come into the market to buy a house less frequently, you may need to talk to each prospect for years before they need you. If you advertised to them two years ago for a one-month period, chances are they're not going to remember you.

Fun fact: the average person will go through more marriages than they will go through cross-country skis! Because Eb's knows how long the buying cycle is for skis, they make every effort to stay top-of-mind, so when someone is finally in the market for cross-country skis, they will automatically think of Eb's. They've been successful in their branding because they have never stopped—they have continually invested in their advertising in order to become a success. And it's working: they've run a successful business for over 40 years.

When it comes to business, there are no quick and easy solutions; advertising success does take time, but it pays off in the form of a profitable, growing business. If that's what you're looking for, it is well worth the time and effort it takes to get it right. And the first step will be to figure out who you are, who you want to attract, and what you want to say to them. We'll get into more detail on that in the next chapter. For now, take a moment to review the homework and answer these questions.

HOMEWORK

1. What feeling do you think is currently associated with your business? What feeling do you want associated with your business?

2. What are the practical reasons that someone would be motivated to buy from you? What are the emotional reasons?

3. Think of the last three messages you sent out to the market. Were they focused on the "what" or the "why"?

4. Who do you want to serve with your business? Is there anything in your business that currently doesn't support this?

Chapter 2

Finding Your Story

"Business is like tennis. Those who serve well, win."

—Ken Blanchard

There is a common perception that advertising as a whole is dead. I hear it a lot, and I disagree. Advertising, in itself, is alive and well. What's dead is the public's willingness to accept *bad* advertising. People are tired of being bamboozled. They don't want to be tricked and bait-and-switched with hard sell, always-on-sale messages. Buying into the hype is what is dying. Consumers are more sophisticated and more educated about the market and products. They see right through that kind of BS. They don't want to be sold, but they do want to be made aware of the products or services that may meet their needs.

The businesses who tell a genuine story about an extraordinary thing they do are the ones cutting through the clutter and building a tribe. The businesses who are clear on who they are, who they mean to serve, and how they mean to serve them are the ones being noticed and growing their business, despite the belief that advertising is dead.

You know that you'll need to stand out. That's why you're reading this book in the first place. But how do you do that? How can you stand apart from all the other businesses in your market and all the other advertising out there? You start by telling your story.

So, let me ask you this: what is the story you want to tell? The following points will help you start to answer this question.

Understand yourself

Before you can figure out the story you want to tell about yourself, you need to understand who you are as a business. You need to know the specifics of what you do—both what your services are and the benefits you offer—who you serve, and the reasons you are in business (your *why*).

What do you do?

Let's start with the question that seems most obvious: what business are you in? Let's start from the very beginning to make sure we're all on the same page when we get into the message you're sending to your customers, so let's start by actually defining what you do:

- Do you sell a product or service?
- Is your business seasonal or year-round?
- Is your business local? National? International? Online?
- Do you fulfill a need or a want?

Depending on which categories your business fits into, you will appeal to different audiences in different ways, and therefore take a different approach to the way you craft your messaging to them. Think about how a dental office might have a different message than, say, an online-only tea emporium. Not only would they have a different geographically targeted audience and different business models, they would also tell different stories and access their audiences differently.

WHY ARE YOU IN BUSINESS?

Your *why* should be the driving force behind your business. When figuring out your why, consider what motivated you to get into this specific business. Often, the reason that you got into business can answer the question, *what solution do you provide for your customers?*

When I asked a group of my business-owner friends why they got into business, they had varying answers. However, the prevailing theme was that they all saw an opportunity to benefit their customers. They wanted to serve customers better, bring them something new, fulfil consumer demand, assist them in a way that nobody had before, make something easier for them, contribute to their growth, balance, and well-being, or make them smile.[1]

Now ask yourself what you love about what you do. When you define what you really love about your business, you can often answer the question, *how do you serve your customers better than anyone else could?*

The point of any kind of advertising and communication is to get people to choose you. Why should customers choose you over your competition? It may be just because you're the loudest with your marketing (especially if you can't seem to find anything that differentiates you), but it's a bigger win if it's because you are actually better. You'll make it easier for the market to distinguish you from one of your competitors; to know how you're different and how you are a better fit for them than your competitors.

Where is the biggest opportunity for you? Where is your market being under-served? What changes in your industry might provide an opening in the market? What other trends are affecting your business right now? What do you see changing soon? You have to look at what the market is doing right now and where it's headed in order to adapt and capitalize on opportunities. When it comes to advertising, staying one step ahead of trends (or at least at the same pace) will help you target your customers at the right times and in the right ways.

SOLVE A PROBLEM

Now that we've gotten into who you are as a business, let's define the problem(s) you solve for your customer. As you read through this section, consider how many of the categories your company fits into. When you look at it from this perspective, you will likely discover solutions you're providing that you were unaware of before.

As an example, Brainsport matches customers with walking and running shoes by spending time with each customer, measuring their feet, and watching how they walk and run so they can recommend shoes that are the right fit. This extra time and attention prevents pain and issues down the line. But what Brainsport is selling is not shoes; it is a comfortable day on your feet at work or a comfortable run without sore hips or shin splints.

Solving a problem for customers is Brainsport's brand and it is why thousands of locals choose them over big box and online stores when they need shoes. Because Brainsport really understands the problems their customers face, they can tell a compelling story about what they do and that brings customers through their doors. Once they are in the store, the experience is what sells the shoes.

It sounds simple, but figuring out the problems you solve isn't always easy. To help you out, here are some common solutions businesses offer to their customers. Try to find where you fit in.

Do you make someone feel included?

When someone comes to your shop, do you make them feel like they belong and that they're one of your tribe? Or do make them feel like they're interrupting your work or that they aren't in the right place?

I was in line at a convenience store the other day. There were five of us in line at one till and the other checkout was closed. Waiting in line isn't the worst thing in the world, but the wait was fairly long. As the line got longer, a young employee came up to the front. We all sighed in relief, knowing the wait would be much shorter once he opened his till to help us out. Except that rather than opening his till, he decided now would be a good time to restock the gift cards and lottery tickets at his lane. Instead of seeing the customers as the main focus of his job, he saw us as an interruption to his restocking duties. Everyone in line just got that much more annoyed—definitely not the best customer experience.

As another example, I have been a member of my local community centre for quite a while and I visit regularly. Most of the staff has also been there for years, but every time I go, they seem to have no recollection of me or my family at all. Because the staff doesn't pay enough attention to even recognize us, it leaves me feeling like an outsider. I'm a repeat customer, but they don't do anything to make me feel like I'm part of their tribe. If there was an alternative in the area, I would likely switch to them because I don't like the feeling I get when no one cares that I've been there before.

When you make an effort to recognize and reward your customers for their continued support, they will start feeling great about your business. The better you make them feel when they visit you, the better chance you have of adding them to your tribe.

Do you make someone's life easier?

The average person in our society is cash rich and time poor. They value things that save them time and are willing to pay for them, so if you offer products and services that do that, you are likely to become successful in your business.

Are you saving them time? Being expedient? Eliminating a commute? If you're the dry cleaner who is saving someone time because you happen to be the closest to where they work or because you deliver cleaned items right to their office, that might be all you need to win business. There's not a lot of difference between your cleaning services and those of your competition, but you are offering convenience to the thousands of people who don't want to go out of their way or who will pay for delivery.

Mobile mortgage brokers are a great example of saving time as they come to your home or work to complete your mortgage transaction. If you have a busy lifestyle, you're more likely to choose someone who is willing to come to you, so they are likely to get more business because they offer convenience to their clients.

Sometimes, you aren't the only one who provides a certain benefit to customers in your market. Maybe every single medical lab in my area has a mobile app. And maybe 15 out of our 20 mortgage brokers are willing to travel to me. But I wouldn't know. Only the businesses who are putting that message out there are going to reap the benefits. If you're the only one talking to the market about that feature, or you have the biggest voice, you will become known for providing that benefit. Even if competitors wake up and start advertising down the line, your "first in" position will give you a huge advantage.

Do you offer something unique?

Offering something no one else offers makes you the only choice when people are looking for that specific thing.

That can be a huge blessing when it comes to developing your message. This is often the case with stores that carry exclusive brands of clothing or footwear, but can apply to service-based businesses as well.

There's a dentist out east that says they specialize in wimps. If you're scared of going to the dentist, they provide many things, including Valium, to help take the fear out of visiting the dentist. Closer to home, my dental clinic has just renovated an area of their office to look like a castle. Who wouldn't want to take their kids to a castle for dental work? A small thing can have a big impact on your potential customers, especially if it's unique.

The trick is to then make sure you tell your customers about it. What good would it do for a dentist to provide anything that makes the experience unique if they don't tell potential patients about it and draw in the people they want to serve?

DO YOU SAVE SOMEONE MONEY?

Perhaps the most obvious problem to solve is the money issue. Most people don't turn down an opportunity to save money, especially if your products are the same or at least comparable to your competitors'.

A great example of this in advertising is Geico's "Fifteen minutes could save you 15% or more on car insurance" campaign. They've taken an unromantic "need" product and offered a benefit that differentiates them from the competition. Not only are they different (and clever!) but they save you money while offering the same products as their competitors.

Saving your customer money doesn't have to mean your products are cheap. It can also mean that you sell a better-quality product for more money upfront, but that lasts longer, saving the customer money in the long-run. Take Buy Me Once as an example: they sell higher end products that they know will last a lifetime. You pay more upfront, but you never have to buy it again. They attract customers who don't like being wasteful, but also people who know that investing in high-quality products means saving money in the long run. So, if you can clearly demonstrate the long-term savings to your customers, it may be an effective way to market yourself. We all learn time and again that you get what you pay for.

When you include the benefit of saving money—either on an equal product or in the long-run—in your marketing, you will hit on a huge pain point for many consumers and drive them right into your store.

BE DIFFERENT

Nobody else can do things quite the way you do. You may have a new way of doing business, a unique product mix, different brand names, or a better location. You may have a specially trained chef, so the pork tenderloin you serve is different than the pork tenderloin at any other restaurant. When you do things differently, you stand out from your competitors.

Meet Precision Auto Body—one of the largest collision repair shops in my community. While most body shops have each of their technicians working on one car's repairs from start to finish, Precision's process follows the Toyota lean production line where each technician only works on one portion of the vehicle's repair.

Precision has streamlined their process of fixing cars, resulting in a more efficient repair and faster turnaround time. They also have the most repair bays in town, so again, they can get more cars through the repair process faster. If I were to ever get into an accident, I'd want my car back as soon as possible and Precision makes it clear that they do that better than anyone else. A company should always be looking for claims they can make to help them stand apart from the competition.

You may have heard of Ellen's Stardust Diner in New York City. It's a 50s-themed diner in downtown Manhattan that is famous for their singing wait staff. While you feast on diner food, you get to be entertained by talented singing waiters, many of whom are supplementing their professional performing income or are up-and-comers who go on to become Broadway or silver screen stars.

My husband and I got to visit Ellen's last fall. After waiting in a lineup that was two blocks long, we got to the door where a bubbly server whisked us in, took our order, and delivered our milkshakes, burgers, and fries to our table with a flourish. He then proceeded to climb up on the back of a booth in the middle of the room to lead the patrons around him in an enthusiastic sing along to "Greased Lightning."

Ellen's has seating for about three hundred people on the ground floor and a balcony that goes around the whole place so everyone can see the middle of the room. One after the other, the wait staff will start a new song and the crowd sings along. They choose songs that everyone knows and loves, so people get into it. When I was telling my publisher about this place, his response was, "Note to self: never go to that place." But he is allergic to fun. For the rest of us, this is a very cool experience. Because of the unique environment at Ellen's, people are willing to stand in that two-block lineup.

Most of us don't have access to Broadway-level talent, nor do we want to sing along to show tunes through every hour that we are at work, but on a smaller scale any business can differentiate themselves by the experience they provide from the minute customers walk through the door. If you put some effort into making sure there is something unique about your offering, the messaging you send out will be stickier and more noticeable.

The problem is that not every business sees themselves as unique. Maybe your business is a family restaurant, or you sell baby clothes. You might think you're just like everyone else, but that's not necessarily true. Here are some ways your business might shine:

DO YOU HAVE A UNIQUE SERVICE?

Perhaps you offer a completely new experience like Ellen's, or maybe you simply have friendlier or more knowledgeable staff. Think about the steps you go through with each customer when they come in. What do you do differently than your competitors?

At the salon I go to, the stylists have assistants who wash your hair, give you a scalp massage, bring you a coffee with flavored creamer, and then offer you a hand massage while your color sets. Other salons have similar prices and quality, but that little bit of extra service is what makes me continue to pick this one. None of these are deal breakers, but they are the details that add a wow factor to the experience.

If there's nothing that differentiates your product from anybody else, then the way to make yourself stand out is with what you do when people come through your doors. The key to success here is to make sure that you repeat the process every single time someone visits so people can count on a consistent experience. And then this becomes another part of your story.

Do you have better staff?

When it comes to customer experience, it's your staff that will make all the difference. They are the ones your customers interact with, so you want to be sure they represent your store the way you want them to. Proper hiring is crucial here. The best employers hire based on the right personality; the technical skills required to do the job can usually be taught (as long as the employee is coachable).

Specialty stores like Eb's and Brainsport hire staff who live the lifestyle their brand represents. That means that when you walk into these stores, you know you will be helped by someone who actually knows what they are talking about, has used the equipment you're buying, and can relate to you personally. Compare that to a store like Walmart, where their focus is on low prices. The customer experience is not their focus and their staff are by no means experts (or even helpful, really).

So, if your staff are experts, or they are simply friendlier and more helpful, this also becomes part of the story you can tell about yourself. Just be sure your staff is actually living up to the expectations you set.

While most employees want to do a good job, it is important that you hire well, and that you make sure you communicate to them who you are and what you stand for. There's nothing worse than choosing a restaurant based on the special promotions their commercials promise, only to have the staff not offer or even be aware of the deals when the customer gets there. It's frustrating to get excited about social media posts that are friendly and happy only to get to the store to find sour-faced staff sitting and engaging with their mobile phones rather than their customers. Your team needs to know what story you're sending out so that they deliver on your promise.

Business owners often blame the advertising for not working when the advertising actually worked and led customers to the business only to find that the staff fail to live up to those expectations. **Advertising works to get people to the door, but it's your job to make the sale once they get there** and provide an experience they want to come back for.

DO YOU HAVE A BETTER SALES PROCESS?

Your sales process is what happens once a customer walks through the doors. When they arrive, do you come right up to them and show them around? Do you leave them be and wait for them to ask for help? A good sales process delivers the experience promised in your branding and advertising.

Brainsport has a fantastic sales process. Rather than walking in, looking at the wall of shoes, choosing the one that you think is prettiest, and having an employee fetch your size for you, they do the following:

1. When you walk in, a salesperson asks what kind of shoes you're shopping for.

2. They ask if you have any issues with pain or injuries, and then they measure your feet.

3. They watch you walk or run so they can see how your feet and body move.

4. They pick out a few pairs of shoes for you to try on and do more checking to make sure your fit is perfect.

5. When you buy the shoes, you can take them home and try them out in real life. If they don't work for you or they cause blisters, you can exchange them for another pair. They don't advertise this part (and the owner loves me for including it here), but it's an important part of their outstanding sales process.

Is your sales process designed to maximize the experience and benefit for your customers and make them raving fans? Or is it set up to pressure them into a quick sale whether it is the right fit or not?

If you have a unique or better sales process, this can be a key part in the story you tell as it enhances the customer experience (and consequently, your brand) and creates those feelings of happiness and satisfaction that customers want to tell their friends about.

CHANGE THE STORY

Okay, so you know who you are as a company, which problems you solve for your customers, and the specifics of what makes you unique in the market. Now, how do we craft the story? Well, we start with the story that's already being told about you. This is the most important part because you need to know what your potential customers already think before you can decide if you should be changing their minds completely, or changing or reinforcing parts of the story.

WHAT ARE YOU CURRENTLY KNOWN FOR?

As a business owner, you are inside the bottle of your business. You know everything there is to know about the business you're in and you are in the middle of it every day. Because you are inside, it can be difficult to see how it looks to people on the outside. It's impossible to read the label from inside the bottle.

If you talked to 10 people at a party and told them what business you own, what response would you get from them? What have they heard about your business? How many have actually heard of your company?

It's important to know how the market currently perceives your business, so you can determine how much work you need to do to get the right story out there. Consider all of the people who aren't shopping at your store: is it because they don't know about you or is it because they do, but they don't like what they hear? What are you known for that you don't want to be known for? Are there misperceptions about your business?

Here are a few ways you can reach people outside the bottle and find out more about what is being said about your business:

- Ask people you meet
- Survey your own employees
- Empower some of your friends to ask on your behalf
- Empower your staff to ask
- Hire a market research company to conduct a survey
- Ask your local college's marketing class to take you on as a project
- Conduct an online survey

Most of the time, this will be a learning process for you. If you've never done this type of research, you'll have to try out different methods and see what works for your particular situation. Market research like this requires you to test, learn, and refine the process as you go—it's always a work in progress. But to kick start your journey, work through this step-by-step guide to find out how your business is perceived in the market:

STEP 1: OUTLINE YOUR OBJECTIVES[2]

Before running out and engaging your customers in a research exercise, it's important to document your objectives. What do you want to learn? Which misperceptions do you want to measure? What information will ultimately help you make decisions about your brand?

Start by making a list of the things you want to discover from the consumer marketplace. This will help set you on the right track. Share your ideas with others involved in the research exercise, so you are all on the same wavelength. In the market research world, there's a saying: "Garbage in, garbage out." If the objectives haven't been properly set out in the beginning, any research you do will come up short.

STEP 2: DECIDE WHAT YOU WANT TO LEARN

Once you know your objectives, you can determine which pieces of information will help you achieve those objectives. If you want to measure misperception, for example, you'll need to know what people are thinking about your business and what they are saying to their friends.

Here are a few other examples of what you might want to learn:

- Level of awareness for your brand and for competitor brands
- Reasons people choose the company with which they do business in your category
- What people think of your company
- What would compel people to try your product or service or visit your store
- Level of awareness and interest in your products' unique features
- Demographic details of those participating in the survey (age, gender, family status, income, and anything else that might be relevant to your business)

STEP 3: DETERMINE WHO YOU WILL ASK

Next, you need to figure out from whom you want to get feedback. Consider how valuable it will be to speak with both current and potential customers. If you are just starting your business, it is important to understand what types of people will likely be most interested in your offering.

This can come in many forms. Perhaps you choose a test market based on the lifestyle you want your brand to associate with, or a certain gender and age group. If you want to appeal to a wide range of customers, you might ask anyone and everyone around you, but if you expect your brand will appeal to a smaller niche, you should look to that specific group as much as possible, since it's their opinions that matter to you most.

STEP 4: SELECT THE METHODS YOU WILL USE

Once you know from whom you want to collect feedback, you must decide how you will solicit their input. Market research is broken up into two types of information: quantitative and qualitative.

Quantitative data will help you understand the lay of the land. It's typically done with a large segment of the market and focuses on measurable data. For example, "x% are aware," "x% would go if…happened," etc. Qualitative research digs deeper and allows you to peel back the layers so you can fully understand purchase motivators, barriers, and their associated emotions. Think of it as having a good chat around a coffee table. Generally, this means you'll be able to reach out to fewer people, but the information you get would be much deeper and more valuable. Depending on what you already know and what you need to know, you may want to collect both qualitative and quantitative information.

For the best results, make an effort to find a balanced mix of opinions and be careful to include a diverse selection of participants rather than a snowball approach where you ask your friends, and their friends, and their friends. A snowball approach narrows the diversity of your respondents and you will likely miss out on many who can share valuable insights about your business. Similarly, only talking to people walking past your business won't offer a balanced sample of the population. Pause and think about multiple ways you can reach your audience for your research.

Some common quantitative research methods include:

- Intercept interviews (approaching people to complete face-to-face interviews)
- Online surveys (pop-up surveys on a website or email invitations if you have a list)
- Telephone (although this method is time consuming and not overly effective if you are conducting the survey yourself)
- Mail-out surveys
- Online analytics (can give you data about visitors to your website and social media platforms)

Some common qualitative research methods include:

- Focus groups (get a small group of people together to chat)
- One-on-one interviews

- Observation research (observe people while they use products or services in your category)
- Mystery shopping your competition (pretend to be a customer and see how they present their products, services, and brand)
- Observing how your customers interact and behave online by paying attention to the conversations your audience is having on social media

Before you jump into your research though, you'll need to develop effective questions to ask your participants.

CRAFTING EFFECTIVE QUESTIONS

How you craft your questions will determine whether or not you get clean, clear, and usable answers from respondents. Ensuring that the proper questions are asked and that they are asked in the right way will be the keys to your success. There is a subtle art to questionnaire design, and you will learn this over time, but here are a few tips get you started:

Include both open-ended and closed-ended questions. Open-ended are the *why* and *how* questions such as, "Why do you shop at x?" or, "How do you decide it's time to start shopping for y?" Answers to these questions help provide context and allow your respondents to tell you more about what they think and how they think about it.

Closed-ended questions are ones in which respondents are provided with a list of options to choose from. These are helpful to quantify information such as, "x% have heard of my business," or, "x% shop at [insert business name]." You will need both styles of questions to get a balanced and effective set of responses.

Avoid biased or leading questions. Don't go fishing for the answer you want to hear. Keep things neutral and generic.

Do not ask two questions at once. Double-barreled questions confuse respondents and provide misleading data. An example of such a question might be, "How would you rate [insert company name] website for being informative *and* easy to use?"

The order in which you ask the questions is important. Use a funnel approach with your questions—start general then work your way down to more specific questions.

Take an insurance agency for example. Here's a sample order in which questions could be asked:

1. What is the first insurance broker that comes to mind? (open-ended question)

2. List any other insurance companies that come to mind. (open-ended)

3. Which agency do you use? [provide a list of prominent businesses] (closed-ended)

4. Why do you choose this company?

5. What is most important to you when choosing an insurance agency?

6. How well is your agency meeting your needs?

7. What sets your agency apart from the rest?

8. Have you ever heard of [insert your company name]?

9. What comes to mind when you think of this company?

10. Why do you / don't you use this company?

11. Are you aware of the following unique attributes of [insert your company name]?

12. Do any of these attributes make you more interested in trying them? Which ones?

Try to keep your questionnaire length to less than five minutes. Once you've developed your questions, ask a sample respondent to complete the questionnaire and measure how long it takes for them to complete it.

Be sure to include questions that reveal the emotional connection people have with the brand they use and how they feel about your brand (if they know you).

WHAT DO YOU WANT TO BE KNOWN FOR?

We started this chapter by asking, "what do you do?" We were talking about general categories of business, but now that we've explored why you are in business, what problems you solve, what makes you different, and what people think of you, let's revisit the question and see if the answer has changed.

When you focus more on your unique attributes and the problems you solve for your customers, the "what" of your business becomes much more remarkable and enticing. Take these as examples:

- A car insurance agency may say that they sell protection from financial loss, but a more effective way to communicate that would be to say that they sell peace of mind on the road.

- A giftware store may say they sell gift items, but it would be more effective to say that the store helps people express their love.

- A coffee shop is your meeting and fueling station.

- A yard maintenance company offers a beautiful yard without the hassle.

- A jewelry store creates unforgettable moments.

If you start thinking about what business you are in based on the core benefit(s) you provide to your customers, it will start to shift your conversations and change the focus of your messaging. This is the first step in telling and changing your story and becoming known for the qualities you want to be associated with.

• • •

As we move toward developing the message you want to send to your potential customers, you will have to understand who you are, who you serve, and what they need and want from you. This will be key to figuring out what you should be saying to your market and how you should be telling your story. Now that we have looked at these factors in greater detail, answer these questions:

1. What do I do?

2. Why does it matter?

3. Who should care?

A one-sentence answer for each will become the foundation of your message to your customers. Each of the clients I work with in my coaching practice must answer these three questions accurately and concisely before we move on to anything else. As a business owner, you need to first know what you do, how it is meant to impact people, and who it is you are trying to impact before you can start effectively communicating with your market. It is important to have a clear message that your staff and customers know and understand. In the next chapter, we will build on this and start to develop in more detail the message you want to send to the public.

HOMEWORK

1. Do you sell a "need" or a "want"?
2. Why did you choose this business?
3. What do you love about the work you do?
4. What does your company do better than anyone else?
5. Where is the biggest opportunity for you?
6. What story is being told about your business in the market right now?
7. What would you like the story to be?
8. What is the biggest misperception about your business?
9. Answer the following questions about your business:
   a. What do we do?
   b. Why does it matter?
   c. Who should care?
10. What have you done today, this week, and this month to share this information with the market?

CHAPTER 3

Relating to Your Customer

"Intellectually, emotionally and spiritually, words are the most powerful force there has ever been. Learn to harness their energy and they will richly reward you with happiness, wealth and honor beyond your dreams."

— Roy H. Williams

Now that we've dissected what business you're in and what you want to be known for, let's figure out what to actually say in your messaging. This starts with understanding more about who you are speaking to and what they expect from you. Then, you can figure out where they are and how to get their attention.

FIGURE OUT YOUR AUDIENCE

Before you develop the phrasing and meaning of your message, you need to know who you are speaking to. Think about it like this: does a globetrotter who hasn't been home in years want the same things as a mom of four who can barely find the time to go to the bathroom alone? Do they communicate the same way? Hang out in the same places? Probably not. So, you need to understand who you are speaking to before you can figure out what you want to say. Here are a few ways you can figure that out:

PICTURE YOUR PERFECT CUSTOMER

Let's take a look at who your ideal customer is. When developing your message, it's useful to think of one individual; someone who represents your ideal customer. We'll focus on what they want and need from you, their lifestyle, and their habits. If you get stuck here, it can help to take a look at the customers you already serve and choose one to keep in mind as you go through this exercise. And if you don't have customers yet, focus on the person you *want* to serve. Then, answer these questions:

What do they do? Don't just look at their job and their income, but understand what they do for fun, where they go on weekends, and what their day-to-day life looks like. Do they spend every free moment they have outside? Do they prefer sitting at home watching Netflix with a glass of wine? Do they have a hectic life with kids and a dog and too many projects on their plate? Find out as much as you can about their life so you can better understand what they like, need, and want from you.

To be clear, we're not looking at this in the context of helping you with merchandising and product development. Instead, we just want to know *what they like, want, and need* so we can better understand who they are and what they look for in a brand. Then you can better define how you can best serve them and craft your messaging so it speaks directly to your customer.

What do they like? Considering the lifestyle of the person you want to attract, find out what they like. Maybe they are an avid cyclist or they love movies. Perhaps they like healthy foods and organic products or they just can't give up their fast food habit. When you know what your customer likes, you are one step closer to crafting the perfect message to reach them.

What do they want? Along those same lines, what is it that they really want out of the products you sell? Are they looking for the lowest prices or the highest quality? Do they want everything in their home to be organic and natural, or do they prefer convenience and quick solutions? When you figure out their burning desires, you can connect with them on those exact things.

What do they need? Of course, it's not all about what they like and want—you also have to know what they really truly need. Do they need a new tech solution to update their dying system? Do they simply need you to point them in the right direction to fix their existing system or are they looking for something brand new? Do they need a custom solution or will stock products work for them?

Note: The best way to find out more about your customers is to talk to them. Find out where they are and get to know them. You can do things like focus groups, interviews, and surveys to get to know more about your people. We'll get into more detail later in this chapter.

DEMOGRAPHICS AND PSYCHOGRAPHICS

When I ask my clients who they target with their advertising, the answer is usually a specific demographic, meaning people who share the same gender, age, marital status, and income level. A typical answer would be, "I'm targeting females between 35 and 50 years old, from dual-income households, who have 2.5 kids."This is a good place to start (though I never am sure how you can have .5 of a kid). Thinking about the age, gender, occupation, and marital status of your typical customer helps you narrow down your market and gives you a jumping-off point for your message, but demographics can't paint the whole picture. They don't give you a good enough idea of how your customers behave. Not all baby boomers want the same things. Not all millennials behave the same way.

What advertisers should be thinking more about are the psychographics. What type of person would your business appeal to? What are their values and beliefs? How do they behave? What are their likes and dislikes? What do they need? Do their values match your company values? While demographics are things that can be seen from the outside, psychographics are the internal attributes.

The reason psychographics are such an important consideration is that demographics can tell us *what* people do, while psychographics tell us *why* they do things. They can help you understand why some people buy from you and others never will. It will also help you craft your message so that it appeals to their motivation to buy. The person in your target group is somebody who feels like they belong with your business, who acts a certain way and identifies as a certain type of person because their values match yours and your branding speaks to who they are.

For example, a comic book store's primary target could be a man who is a self-proclaimed nerd. He has a huge collection of comic books and nerd culture paraphernalia, goes to comic book conventions, and potentially owns more than one grown-up-sized superhero costume that is worn more often than just to Halloween parties. However, he doesn't fit within a certain demographic. He could be 22 or 56, unemployed or make six figures, married or single. His demographics could be anywhere, but his values match those of the comic book store.

When you start to think about the psychographics of your customers, rather than just their demographics, you realize that your target market is much bigger than you thought and much easier to reach than you expected.

There is a religious supply and giftware store in my city and I got a chance to chat with the manager about her business. They had always been narrow in their targeting by advertising only in church bulletins and Christian publications. They wanted to attract more customers, but seemed to have hit a glass ceiling with the advertising they had been doing. It's a huge store full of gifts, paintings, home décor accessories, toys, books for all ages, apparel, and jewelry—some with religious messages and others without.

When we got around to talking about the reasons customers are likely shopping there, we touched on several groups they hadn't paid much attention to: people invited to confirmations and first communion celebrations who need a gift but don't go to church themselves, people who like to change up their home décor regularly, and parents who share the ideals and morals present in the kids' books and toys, but don't necessarily attend church or read religious publications. Basically, this store had a much broader appeal than they gave themselves credit for. They were so narrow in their targeting that they were missing other markets that were right in front of them.

When you think beyond simple demographics, you can find out much more about the people who might want to do business with you and open up markets you hadn't thought about.

BUSINESS USE FACTORS

How do people use your business? Why do they come through your doors? Do they come to celebrate something? Are they there to spend time with family? Do they come in for entertainment or necessity? What do they typically do when they get there?

If customers come to your business for a variety of reasons, it might be necessary to craft your message differently for each use. For example, Sardinia Restaurant could just target families with young kids. But they would be missing out on a few different viable market segments that way. I have met clients for lunch there, taken my kids in for pizza on a busy weeknight, and hosted a radio station promotion in their private dining room. By crafting different messages toward multiple uses, you invite people to think of you when any of those situations arise—not just the obvious ones.

THE TROUBLE WITH TARGETING TOO MUCH

In direct sales—and when you have a very small budget— you want to focus on niche markets to ensure that 100% of your effort and budget is going to reach those most likely to buy. However, when it comes to advertising on a bigger scale (on mass media), narrowing down your target audience too much can leave you with more problems than it solves.

Say your target demographic is a female, age 35–50, married, dual-income household. Let's call the people in this demographic Customer A. What possible problems could we run into if we narrow our target this much?

1. It is next to impossible to pay to reach only the Customer A's in your community. You will end up either narrowing your reach too much or being frustrated because you can't figure out how to reach *just* the customer you have described. No mass media is targeted only to Customer A.

2. You are discounting all of the Customer B's, C's, D's who may be attracted to your business. By casting a tiny, Customer A-sized net, you aren't even giving yourself a chance to catch any other fish.

3. You are assuming that Customer A's all live in a vacuum; that they are not influenced by anyone else when making a decision. But in reality, the thing that often tips the scale for us when we are making a purchase decision is when someone we know makes a recommendation. So, if Customer C has heard of you and has a good feeling about you, he might tell Customer A about you and that could be the message that actually makes her decide to buy from you.

When I was working in media, one of my clients was a manufacturer who was struggling to recruit welders. They had been advertising jobs in trade magazines for welders and they ran job postings in the "help wanted" section of the newspaper and on recruitment websites asking applicants to stop by their Saturday job fairs. They were only targeting welders, and more specifically, welders who were actively looking for a job. When we met, they were planning another fair.

I set them up with a week of advertising on the local pop radio station because it reached a huge portion of the general population. How many welders could you reach with a pop radio station, you may ask? The organizers were thrilled with the results. With their trade magazines and job postings, they normally saw about 5–10 applicants at their job fairs. After the one-week radio campaign, they saw over 80 applicants that Saturday!

When the staff asked visitors how they heard about the fair or why they stopped by, the answers were, "My girlfriend told me about it," "My mom told me," etc. The people who knew welders amplified the effect of the advertising by telling them about the fair. And significantly, many of the most qualified applicants were welders who were successfully working somewhere but heard about the opportunity and it appealed to them enough to stop by. They never would have been looking in the "help wanted" section of the paper or on a job posting website. The manufacturer cast a bigger net and they caught more fish.

This is what you should strive to do with your advertising as well. You will see bigger, better results when you cast a wider net because you can reach all sorts of potential customers *and* their friends and family who might tell them about it.

HOW FOCUSED SHOULD YOUR TARGET BE?

When considering how focused your target should be, the first question you need to ask yourself is how targeted your product is. Are you a quilting supply store who will literally only appeal to commercial and hobby quilters? Or are you a cupcake shop who... well let's face it...who doesn't like cupcakes? As you can imagine, a quilting store would need to have a much narrower target than a cupcake shop. They could be successful by advertising in only quilting magazines and targeting quilters online, while a cupcake shop could advertise anywhere (and everywhere). Your business will likely fall somewhere between a quilting supply store and a cupcake shop. You may have specialty items, but you'll likely appeal to a variety of people for a variety of uses.

The second question to ask is how much money you have budgeted to spend on advertising. If you have a small budget, you need to target more narrowly, but when you have more money to work with, you can and should cast a bigger net. The scale goes all the way from ads targeted to a small, narrow demographic on social media, to high frequency campaigns on mass media. (We'll talk more about budgets in Chapter 6.)

Narrowing your reach more than necessary limits your opportunity to make impressions on potential customers. I spoke with a specialty renovation supply store recently who was advertising on YouTube. He chose to run his ads just on computers registered in postal (zip) codes in older areas of our city because he figured they were more likely to be candidates for renovations. He also narrowed even further to homeowners between 30 and 60 years of age. That seems pretty reasonable until you think about how many people really fall into all of these categories.

He was only making impressions on home owners in the areas he had targeted who also happened to be in that age demographic, who also watched YouTube *and* happened to catch his advertisement at the beginning of the video they wanted to watch. And only a fraction of those people would need renovation supplies right then.

Our city only has 300,000 people, so you have to ask, how many people will actually be exposed to his message and is that worth the resources he has put into this strategy? His approach may be a great fit in a city the size of Chicago, because in a city of 2.7 million people, targeting 30–60 year olds in older neighborhoods will give you a much bigger pool of people. But in our city, my friend would have been better off using traditional mass media and reaching a larger pool of people, especially since he had a budget that would allow it.

So the products you sell and the overall size of your market will both dictate how narrowly you should be targeting. Generally, you want to advertise as widely as your budget allows you to on a consistent basis. When you cast a bigger net, you will catch more fish.

When you target a large audience, you will be reaching more than just your "ideal customer." What you say in your message will resonate with the people who you're trying to appeal to, and they will identify themselves and say, "Oh, they're talking to me right now." If you're trying to reach the masses, that's where media comes in. You're never going to convert them all, but you don't need them all anyway. Within the large pool of people you reach, there will be more than enough to grow your business, because more than enough people will hear or see it and say "Yes, this is for me." Serve them with everything you have, and don't worry about the rest.

WHAT DO YOU PEOPLE WANT FROM ME!?

David Ogilvy is hailed as "The Father of Advertising," and was a founding partner of Ogilvy and Mather, one of the world's foremost marketing agencies. Ogilvy worked for George Gallup, founder of the Gallup Poll, for many years and learned from him the value of knowing what your customer is thinking. His main message was that you cannot write an advertising message unless you know who you're writing it for, how the customer thinks, and what the customer needs. If you haven't done your research, then you're just faking it, and it'll get you into trouble.

So how do you know what will motivate customers to buy? This section offers ways to get a better idea of what people are looking for, and will help you formulate the message that will compel them.

Most easily and obviously, you can start by asking people who are already shopping with you to find out why they're coming in. Their motivation to support your business may be completely different from what you think it is. For example, you might think people come back to your store month after month because of the products and brands you carry, but with further research, you find that it's actually because your staff does a certain thing every time they come in, or because they remember customers' names, or whatever the case is. So rather than just making assumptions about what your customers like about you, ask them! You can also use this approach to find out what they wish you would carry or a service they want you to offer.

To truly understand the consumer psyche, you need to get a glimpse inside their hearts and minds. Extensive research shows that consumers rarely base purchase decisions on rational factors. As illustrated in our family's choice of a puppy, emotions play a much larger role in the decision of what to buy and who to buy from.

In Chapter 2, we talked about doing market research to find out what people think of your company. You can use some of these same methods and tips to better understand your current client base. To further grasp what your customers experience when they walk through your doors, map their experience and do some analysis.

MAP THE EXPERIENCE[1]

Journey mapping is simply building a step-by-step process of the purchasing experience that starts when a customer first identifies a need for what you sell and ends when they use your product or service. When you identify the process your customers go through, you can understand how and why they come to you. With further analysis, you can use this data to inform your message and marketing tactics as well. It can help you take information you already know and break it down into meaningful chunks.

Of course, there is more than just one path that consumers take. You could go into detail on all sorts of processes and journeys your customers could follow, but don't get caught up in every single detail of every single possible journey— you don't need that. Stick to just a few scenarios at first and see what kinds of insights you can get.

The following is a sample map to show you how it works. Imagine you're a florist. How does someone decide they need to buy flowers from you? Let's look at what Doug might do:

1. Doug is going on a date with his wife, so he decides to buy her a bouquet of flowers.

2. Doug's mind first comes up with top-of-mind flower shops. He considers their pricing, location, product selection, product quality, staff knowledge and, ultimately, brand perception. If the top-of-mind shops meet his needs, he skips Step 3.

3. Doug does some research to find the flower shops in his area. This could be a Google search, asking friends, or looking in the phone book.

4. He chooses the one shop that seems the best to him and proceeds to the store.

5. First impressions are important. Upon entry, Doug subconsciously notices the smells, sounds, colors, merchandising, and staff greeting.

6. He starts his visit with a self-serve evaluation of options and considers what to buy.

7. Staff engage him (either they approach or he approaches them). This can include the usual sales process: assess needs, present options, ask for the sale.

8. Doug makes his selection then waits while his purchase is packaged up and gets advice on how to care for his flowers.

9. Since they are a gift, Doug chooses a card at the checkout and attempts to compose an emotional message in a public place in a compressed time frame on a business-card sized space.

10. He then pays for his flowers. This is his point-of-sale experience (time in line, credit card experience, etc.)

11. Doug takes the flowers home to his wife. His experience might include challenges of preserving their condition in his car, exposure to sub-zero temperatures, etc.

12. When he arrives home, he presents the flowers to his wife and shares all those good emotions.

13. He helps her place the flowers in a vase and follows the steps to preserve them.

14. Doug finds a place for the flowers in their home and he and his wife continue to enjoy and care for the flowers and the symbolic representation of the reason Doug bought the flowers in the first place.

15. Eventually, the flowers die and Doug has to dispose of them.

As you can see, the journey mapping process can be very detailed. As much as possible, consider every single step in the process so you can better understand what your consumers go through when they shop at your store. Don't forget some of the "invisible" steps, like what they do *before* they walk through your doors, or how they might transport their purchase home, or what the person will do *after* using your product.

ANALYZE YOUR MAP

Once you know *what* your customer does, you can further examine what that means to you. Start by first identifying pain points within the process. For a husband buying his wife flowers, it could be feeling intimidated as to what his spouse would appreciate or want. There are so many options and he may feel like he is terrible at this and needs help from a staff member who makes him feel comfortable discussing the options. It isn't as uncomfortable as buying lingerie for his wife, but it isn't like picking up milk on the way home, either. Walk through the journey map and find out what could make your customer's experience better.

In addition to finding opportunities to improve your customer experience, try to understand your customers' motivations and barriers to buying. This overlaps a bit with their pain points, but it looks at the broader psychological decisions they make. Where does the decision start? What needs are you addressing? And how do they choose who to do business with? Once you know what motivates *and* prevents customers from purchasing from you, you can capitalize on this information to change your message, neutralize barriers, and influence decision making.

I know this is not the simplest thing to do, but these tips will help you along the way:

- **Focus on emotions.** Once you understand these, you know how people feel and, therefore, how to influence their motives.

- **Understand the role your product plays in consumer's lives.** This helps provide context about needs and desires to buy.

ANSWERING QUESTIONS NOBODY IS ASKING

As a business owner, you know everything there is to know about your business. Because of this, it's hard for you to sort through all of the information you *could* be telling people and choose what you *should* be telling people. As a result, your advertising can end up filled with too many facts about what you do and how you do it, rather than the benefits you are offering. Don't tell me how many years you've been in business unless that experience makes you uniquely qualified to fill my need better than your competition. Don't tell me your hours of operation unless your extended hours are more convenient for me. Don't tell me the 10-step process you use to clean the carpets in my home, just tell me that your method gets my carpets cleaner with less drying time so my household can be back to normal sooner.

When creating your message, always think of the acronym WIIFM (What's In It For Me)—this is what your audience is asking and should be the main point of your message. What's in it for your audience to listen to the rest of your ad or read the rest of your post, or let you interrupt their day? Rather than reading your resume, listening to your presentation, and hearing your whole history, people really just want to know what you can do for them, how much it will cost, and how they can get it.

LISTING THE BRANDS YOU CARRY

Often, advertisers want to include a list of the brands they carry. Normally, this is unnecessary and simply takes up expensive real estate in your ads. However, there are two situations in which brands should be included in your messaging:

1. When they are brands that people specifically seek out, like designer clothing and footwear. If you carry more of the popular brands, or are the exclusive carrier of those brands, it will benefit you to mention them because it will differentiate you from your competition.

2. When listing the brands would position your business in a beneficial way. For example, if your messaging needs to get across that you are a high-end appliance store, you would talk about the fact that you carry Miele and Thermador to differentiate you from the stores that carry the more mainstream Whirlpool or Maytag.

If no one knows the brands you carry, or you only carry brands that everyone else carries, don't waste the space. Brands in your ads are only meaningful if they have a known value attached to them, or if they are exclusive.

GETTING THEIR ATTENTION

The point of advertising is to stimulate interest in your business. You want to be able to connect with your audience, tell them you're there, and get them to take a step toward you. More often than not, you don't need to educate them on your product line or tell them your whole story. Instead, you just need to get their attention and get them to take some action.

Of course, if it's a new product category that's never existed, then you will have to explain the product a bit. However, most educational ads don't directly serve your business, but your business category as a whole, which ends up benefitting your competitors just as much as it does you. Instead, all of the detailed information you are tempted to list on your ads should simply be placed on your website where people can find it when they are ready.

THINK OF ADVERTISING AS THE FIRST DATE

On a first date, what do you do? Do you immediately jump into talking about getting married and having a family? Not likely. Instead, you tell a short version of your story and get the other person interested enough to take another step with you—your second date.

Ads are just like first dates in that they are not designed to get every person who sees them on board with your company and turn them into loyal tribe followers. Instead, they are there to get your potential clients to take the next step with you. So, you share a snippet of your story and invite them to your website or into your store to get more information and become more familiar with you.

There is no room in a good ad to give too many details and you don't want to overwhelm first-timers. If you're using a billboard, you have five words or less to tell the viewers why they should care to remember your business. Do you sell gardening supplies? Do you offer delicious catering with vegan options? That's as much information as you have time for.

Then, if the viewer decides they need to know all your different menu items and if you deliver on weekends, they can call you or stop in or go to your website. But they are not ready to have all that information thrown at them in a short ad. All they need for now is to know why they should look further. Giving people too much, too soon will make you lose them. Until they have some interest in doing business with you, they don't care about the details.

SALIENCE

Salience is how noticeable, important, or prominent something is. How quickly your message will get noticed is directly proportional to how salient your message is.

Think about the most memorable things that have ever happened to you. You remember the moment you first saw your newborn baby and the way your wife smiled on your wedding day. You remember vividly where you were and what you were doing when you heard that a jet had crashed into the Twin Towers on 9/11, or when you found out a loved one had passed away (or for me, when I heard that

Michael Jackson had died…and of course the birth of my children as well!). These events are the most salient in your world. Everything else you learn or hear falls somewhere lower down on the salience chart.

Your message is less relevant than those major life and world events, so it will take longer to make an impact with people. Memory is equal to salience times repetition, so it will take repetition of your message before somebody will internalize what you're telling them. When you run a branding commercial one time, or for one week, and expect everyone to drop what they're doing and come shop at your store, you're assuming that your commercial is right up there with the moment they met their baby!

Creating the most salient message possible will reduce the frequency with which they need to see your message before they remember it. That's where it becomes important that you create a message that your audience will identify with. The more your message matters to your audience, the more salient it is going to be. If it is clear that you are making their life easier, you're saving them time, you're saving them money, you're making them feel like they'd be part of your tribe, you're making them feel happier, prettier, or cooler, your message will get noticed.

There's a bar in New York's East Village called Please Don't Tell (PDT). Despite the name, a relative had told me about it. When my husband and I visited New York for the first time, visiting PDT was on our itinerary. We found the address online before we left home (this was before the days of smartphones) and sought it out at the end of day one.

Getting to PDT required that we take a subway to the East Village then walk, and walk, and walk, from the subway stop. We (I) had had a very successful shopping day and we (I) had quite a few bags that we were (he was) carrying. We arrived at the address we'd written down, and there was nothing there. I was cranky and hungry and tired from carrying those darn shopping bags. Where we expected to see Please Don't Tell, all we saw was a typical New York apartment with a greasy burger joint downstairs. My husband said, "Let's just leave," but I said, "No. Let's ask."

See, women ask for directions if they can't find things; men just give up. So, we went downstairs to the burger joint and I said, "This isn't Please Don't Tell, is it?" The cook said, "No," and pointed to an old-fashioned phone booth against the wall over by the tables. I walked over to it, stepped in, picked up the phone, and heard someone say, "Please Don't Tell." "Um, hi, can we come in?" I said. Then **the inside wall of the phone booth opened**, revealing a beautiful, dark wood and leather booth-filled restaurant with a girl in a black dress shaking martinis behind a huge bar. There happened to be two seats available.

We settled in, shopping bags crammed around our feet, and ordered drinks. We enjoyed the evening over the most amazing cocktails, and to top it off, the burgers we ordered came from next door's burger joint and were passed through a little secret door in the wall into the bar! After walking in circles to find it, the burgers and cocktails we ordered were the best things we've ever tasted. The story of Please Don't Tell is so interesting that everyone who visits wants to tell it! That's the salient secret to their success.

This place is so memorable and unique that the experience sticks into peoples' minds. I can't tell you every store I shopped at that day (it's been a while!), but I still remember every detail of PDT and I have told dozens of people about it.

Salience is key to a successful advertising campaign. In fact, when David Ogilvy studied the effect of money spent in advertising versus the results of that advertising, in nearly every case, the companies that spent more money enjoyed a bigger market share. However, there were exceptions. In cases where advertisers spent less but got better results, the advertising was so successful in part because they had a more appealing (or salient) message. So, you can get the biggest market share by spending the most money on advertising, but you can get more bang for your buck (better ROI) if you are able to create advertising that is more memorable than your competitors.

• • •

Out of all the elements that form your story, the ultimate goal is to connect with your customers and let them know about the elements of your uniqueness that will benefit them the most. Once you understand your audience and the process they go through in choosing you as their store or brand, you can figure out how to streamline the process and target the emotions and decisions that will bring them through the door.

It's tempting to list a great deal of information in your ads because one thing might pop out at someone and bring them into the store, but what you really want to do is develop a clear and concise story snippet that catches their attention and inspires them to take you on a second date.

In Chapters 4 and 5, we will get into the details of which advertising vehicles work best to achieve different objectives and how you can put together meaningful ads that enhance salience and attract more of the right people to your business.

HOMEWORK

1. What are the demographics of your typical customer?

2. Who are they and what are they about? Think about their lifestyle, their preferences, and their interests (the psychographics).

3. Create a journey map of a typical customer who visits your business. Can you identify any common pain points in the process your customers go through? What would be some simple steps you can take to improve their experience?

4. People buy on benefits, not on features—building on consistency and frequency—what is it about your story that is most likely to compel prospects to take action? What do your customers care about?

5. How do these benefits compare to those of your three main competitors?

CHAPTER 4

Developing Your Message

"Creativity is intelligence having fun."

—Albert Einstein

Every day, we are hit with thousands of branding messages. You wake up in the morning, pick up your phone, scroll past or get distracted by a Facebook ad featuring kids playing hockey. Then you peek at your email and see the latest Michaels coupon in your inbox. When you get out of bed, you use your Bumble and Bumble shampoo in the shower and your Colgate toothpaste at the sink.

When you head downstairs for breakfast, you turn on your Keurig for coffee and see your teenage son watching an ad before his video can play on YouTube on his Apple computer. Your husband has the TV dialed in to the local morning news sponsored by that flooring store that's been around for 30 years.

You get in your car, listen to your favorite radio morning show, and hear two commercial breaks before you get to work; one with a donut shop commercial that tempts you to stop on your way to work, and one for the sidewalk sale happening this weekend at the mall.

At that really long stoplight you hate, you wait behind a bus wrapped in an ad for a realtor who surely can't still look like that because he's run that same photo of himself for the last 10 years. Your eyes catch three flashing digital billboards before you turn off the main drag; one for the caterer who does wedding cakes, one for the Ford dealership, and one for something you can't read because there are too many words in small font. For a split second, you wonder what it was, but you quickly give up on it.

As you pull into the parking lot at the shop, you see an employee's truck that has a license plate with your favorite football team's logo on it and that tiny red hatchback with the radio station sticker on the back window.

You haven't even walked into work yet and you have been exposed to over 50 brands.

How do all these brands cut through the clutter and make a lasting impression on you? You didn't actively think about or register every single one of them this morning, but the sum total of all of their activities over your lifetime should make you familiar with the ones who do the best job of staying in your path. The information overload we are hit with is like aiming a fire hose at a teacup. Very little of what is thrown at us can be retained. What can *you* do to be the small amount of water that will stay in the cup?

Tim Hortons is an iconic Canadian brand. It's a coffee and donut shop, but what a Canadian thinks when the Tim

Hortons name comes up is warmth, pride in being Canadian, outdoor hockey rinks, bringing the comfort of home to our military overseas, and welcoming newcomers. It's a warm and fuzzy brand and it is synonymous with Canadian culture. Did this happen because of one commercial or campaign? No. It comes from years of impressions sent through all the different media with that consistent feel and core message.

How about Colgate? Toothpaste is something we rarely think about—certainly not when we are trying to keep our eyes open while squeezing paste onto our toothbrush at 6 am—but when we are standing in the aisle at the grocery store, Colgate stands out among the dozens of toothpaste options because we have a feeling of trust and seem to remember that at least 3 out of 4 dentists would tell us to buy it.

Because of information overload, we have to make sure that our ads are interesting. They need to be as salient as possible, so we should aim to surprise and delight our audience and entertain while we persuade. That does not necessarily mean coming up with crazy stunts in hopes that the video footage will go viral online. It means saying *no* to predictable words, overly straightforward copy, and cluttered layout, and saying *yes* to telling a story, painting a picture, and appealing to emotion. If you do this, you will gain the attention of your audience and create salience in your messaging.

If I were you reading this for the first time, I'd be thinking, "What the hell!? I'm not a writer or a designer! How am I supposed to come up with an ad that will do these things?" So, if that's where your mind is going, I get it.

But unless you are planning to sky-write your message out of the back of your own plane, you are likely working with a digital marketing company, some sales reps from local media, or an ad agency. So rather than teaching you all about ad creation and design, this chapter aims to arm you with the information you'll need to have more meaningful conversations with those responsible for your creative messaging.

Often, when you meet with your marketing team, you will find yourself getting caught up talking about ad placement, volume, budget, media mix, and schedule. The message itself is often a last-minute add-on when someone says, "What do you want to put in your ad?" Or even, "I'll have the writer call you and you can send him the points you want to cover." Leaving it to the end implies that what you say is not as important. But oh my gosh, it is *so* important! It may be the *most* important!

When you have a compelling enough message, it should really work anywhere. Failing to focus on the message itself is often why advertising comes up short. It's not because your ad didn't reach a viable audience, it's because you weren't able to convince them to care about what you had to say.

Representing your brand

When it comes to representing your brand, what you say and how you say it are even more important than the vehicle(s) you choose. In Chapter 2, we looked at finding your story and developing the brand that represents who you are as a business. Then in Chapter 3, we focused on who your audience is and what they want. Now, you'll take what you've learned and start applying it to your advertising.

As we look at the possible ways to tell your story and reach your customers, remember who you are and what your audience wants and needs as you're crafting your ads. It's up to you to decide which elements will work with your message and which ones won't.

WRITING AN AD

As an advertiser, you need to resist the temptation to get too creative and off-the-wall with your ads, **especially if your creativity comes at the expense of clarity**. Although creativity can be memorable, sometimes it's okay to have an informational ad that clearly states who you are, what you sell, and ultimately, why the audience should care. One of the most talented writers I've ever worked with says that your radio ad should serve as your "audio business card," that gently, professionally, and consistently invites people to do business with you. Finding the right balance of information and creativity will yield the best results.

When it comes to ads, though, no one wants theirs to sound like an ad. When I was in the radio business, we would hear this… All. The. Time. Of course, you want to stand out and be noticed, but making every ad on a station sound like *not* an ad is a pretty difficult task—and it's not necessary. Going too far off in left field without including a persuasive sell message may be entertaining to the audience, but will it sell your product?

I was working with a woman who owns a home building company. She had hired an agency to arrange her media advertising. When I sat down to work out the radio advertising with the agency rep, the first thing the rep said was, "We want to be out of the box. Different. We don't want the ad to sound like an ad." He shared with me that our client was a huge fan of Harry Potter. He thought it would be great to run an ad that sounded like a scene from the movies, somehow featuring the business name, then a tag at the end about our client's home building company.

The thing is, nobody had heard about this home builder yet. She had a lot of unique business attributes that would immediately appeal to potential customers if they were communicated, but up to that point she had done *no* advertising. Nobody knew that her company existed! If we went ahead with this Harry Potter idea for our "non-commercial commercial," we wouldn't have had a chance to get across her basic differentiators and the way she was going to serve her clients.

Instead, we began with a more traditional ad to start out with. I explained that once she had established her brand and her name was in the minds of her potential customers, she could start getting more creative with what she was doing. And that is the advice I continue to give—start off simple. Focus on your unique selling points and the benefits you offer your clients, then get creative.

That being the case, we don't want to bore the audience. There are some creative elements that can work well and add to the salience of your message.

PAINTING THE PICTURE

You have a better chance of inspiring someone to act if you can first get them to picture themselves doing what you want them to do. Once they've imagined it in their minds, they're more likely to follow through and actually do it. So, if you get your potential customer to imagine herself paddling on a glass-calm lake at dusk in the middle of July with just the sound of loons to keep her company, she is more likely to buy that paddle board from you because she wants to make that dream become a reality.

Here is an example of an audio commercial that paints the picture:

Background sound effect: crackling fire

Where shadow meets fire. Where upscale meets laid back. Where gastro meets pub. A delicious meal? Drinks with friends? Break bread—at The Royal Oak. Stop in for a drink at the Royal Oak. The glimmering bronze row of the very best scotch and bourbon bottles greet you from behind the bar as you walk by. A dark ale being poured into a frosty glass. Cozy on in to the leather booth and feel the warmth of the fire as you take your first sip while the chatter of patrons and the faint jazz music hum around you. The Royal Oak. Now open proper pub hours, downtown on 2nd Avenue.

This ad makes you imagine how it would look, sound, and feel when you visit the business. And, of course, that makes you want to experience it for yourself.[1]

USING HUMOR

A great way to surprise or delight your audience is to make them laugh. Humor is one of the best ways to get and keep your audience's attention and can improve their overall feeling toward your brand. It's most effective for products that people have to think about the least and that cost the least amount of money (like food, alcoholic beverages, toys). The keys to success with humor are to make sure that it is appropriate for the product and audience, and that it ties into the products it's promoting.

Having said that, it is very difficult to get humor right, and copywriters generally *hate* you when you say, "I want something funny," because copywriters are not standup comics, and forced comedy usually turns out badly. With humor, you run the risk of being the ones that tried to be funny and failed. It's also the scariest style to try in advertising. You don't want to entertain without the sell message sticking in the minds of your audience, and humor gets old fast; funny campaigns need to be updated or revised regularly to keep them alive. Plus, even though funny ads get attention, studies show that they don't increase product recall or purchase intention any more than other styles of ads.

Super Bowl ads create a buzz every year and they are often looked at as benchmarks for the funny, moving, or iconic. And while they are often memorable for their entertainment value, they have not shown to result in increased sales in the majority of cases. When they go for over $4M per 30-second spot, that's a lot of money to spend just to entertain. Some would say that the companies who buy time during the Super Bowl gain more value from teasing the ad leading up to the event and the bragging rights of saying they have an ad in the Super Bowl than from the commercial itself.

One of my favorite Super Bowl commercials was the "The man your man could smell like" ad from 2010; and it is a good example of humor done right. This one still makes me laugh every time I watch it. Memorable lines from the ad include, "It's two tickets to that thing you like," and "I'm on a horse." You remember that this was a commercial for Old Spice, don't you? Because the whole ad was focused on your man being the man you want him to be because he smells good. Old Spice went on to produce more ads that were just as funny and persuasive in that series, being one of the few that effectively pulled off humor in advertising.

A fantastic example of a local business using humor is an ad series from Precision Auto Body. They developed a character named Rocco who was based on the owner's Italian uncle. Rocco became the voice of their radio commercials as a playful jokester who implores the audience to go see his buddy Joe at Precision Auto Body when they've been in an accident. They've had scenarios like the aftermath from a shopping cart hitting a car in the parking lot, Rocco interviewing the staff at the shop, a car looking like it went back in time to the day it was born, and even Rocco reporting on the traffic conditions from up in his "chopper" ("Rocco that's just you beating your hands on your chest!").

Each message focuses on ensuring the audience knows they will get your car fixed "fasta, fasta, more fast" and looking like brand new. They continue to run their company jingle in the background with the business name and tagline sung at the end. These ads get customers talking and looking forward to hearing what Rocco will get up to next. Some people have even said they chose to bring their car to Precision specifically because of Rocco.

Humor is one way to surprise and delight, but it is difficult to do well and it's challenging to effectively relate the humor to the product or service being advertised. If you can get it right, it can be great for businesses, just don't try to force it. You don't *have* to be funny if that's not what feels right to you or if it's just not working.

KEEPING IT PROFESSIONAL

Sometimes the desire to be creative and stand out goes a bit too far and can be inappropriate, especially for certain business categories.

A few years back, a financial planner ran a full-year campaign on the radio. He really wanted to be funny, so the ads were based around a couple of goofy characters. In the entire year, he could not credit one single lead as coming from those ads, which is almost unheard of for a year-long campaign.

The thing is, hiring a financial planner requires a lot of trust because you're dealing with your life's savings. You're not likely to say, "Haha…okay you're hilarious! All kidding aside, though, here's all my money." A financial planner, just like a realtor, mortgage broker, or lawyer, needs to come across as totally professional, competent, and in control of the situation. So being too goofy and cute can backfire.

If you're not sure which way to go, think about your customer's journey map. What do they look for in a business in your industry? What do your ideal clients like and appreciate? If they are likely a serious bunch when shopping your category, or if you need to inspire trust and confidence, stick with a more professional tone.

BEING SPECIFIC

When it comes to selling, details and specific outcomes are more persuasive than generalities. Instead of telling your customers you can fix their car quickly, tell them how quickly. That helps the idea stick and lets them know they can trust what you're saying.

Which of these would be more impactful?

- "We fix your car faster," or, "We fix your car in 48 hours or less."
- "We offer big savings on printer cartridges," or, "We sell printer cartridges for 30% less than the big box stores."
- "The store has a great selection of shoes," or, "The store has 500 styles of designer shoes."
- "Our branches are open extended hours," or, "We're open 'til midnight every night."

Whenever you can, quantify your claims with specifics. As long as you can deliver on the promise every time, being specific will enhance your message and clearly show the benefits you offer.

STAYING CONSISTENT

In Chapter 3, we looked at the idea of your ads being the "first date" with your customers. You don't want to give too much away or require too much of a commitment from your ads, because the next step should be to visit your website or walk into your store. But what happens when they actually do come in?

Because you know your ultimate goal is to get people through your doors, think of your ad as a promise of what the experience will be when your customers visit you. If you have a fun and upbeat ad, customers will expect you to have a fun and upbeat store. You don't want your customers to be caught off guard, so keep your ads consistent with your atmosphere.

Because Alex from Sardinia Restaurant makes everyone feel welcome and like part of his family, we translated this restaurant culture into the commercials we ran. We used Alex's voice in the ads, welcoming customers just like he does in person. The ads were very effective, as they were consistent with the warm, inclusive feeling customers experience in the restaurant. When new customers came to the restaurant, it was exactly what they expected, so they were more likely to be comfortable and happy to be there.

SURPRISING YOUR AUDIENCE

Another way to gain attention for your ad is to surprise your audience. Instead of running the same old ads and doing everything exactly the same as your competitors, try going in a unique direction—especially if you don't differ very much from your competition in other ways.

I was asked to develop an advertising campaign for a Chinese food restaurant located in a residential neighborhood in the north end of the city. There were no specific dishes that were unique to this place and they didn't have a notable chef or any other distinguishing feature that we could use to help them stand out. They simply served good Chinese food. When I took the dilemma to my copywriter, he said, "Leave it with me," and came back with a brilliant angle.

Instead of starting the ad with the sound of a gong followed by Chinese music in the background and a list of their dishes like you would expect, the commercial sounded like it was for the coolest nightclub in New Orleans. It had funky slow music in the background and a low, honey-like voice that talked about the restaurant serving Chinese soul food. It had straightforward information, but it surprised and delighted the audience because it took an unexpected approach to the delivery.

We used this creative approach and focused the message on their location and late night delivery. Because the ad itself was completely different than what people expected, the campaign actually worked well, despite not having a unique benefit to focus on.

MASCOTS AND CHARACTERS

Characters and mascots have represented brands for decades. Tony the Tiger represents Frosted Flakes cereal, the Michelin Man sells tires, and Mr. Clean promotes household cleaning products. These characters work because they personify the message that these brands want to send. Frosted Flakes are kid-friendly. Michelin tires are safe and reassuring like this big soft character. Mr. Clean's powerful cleaning products will make your house sparkle. The reason these work is because the characters make it easy for the brands to illustrate their benefits. For unsexy commodity products, these characters have helped differentiate their brands from all the other choices.

For small businesses, a character can become the face and voice of a business on TV, in print, online, and on the radio. Aim Electric is a great example. They are an electrical company that offers residential, commercial, and industrial electrical services. The radio station's creative department developed a character called Big Kenny to be the spokesperson for Aim.

Big Kenny is a gentle, low-voiced grandfatherly farmer-type guy, and he "tells it to you in real speak" when he talks about the things Aim Electric just installed or repaired on his farm. Big Kenny has talked about the guys at Aim Electric in all different scenarios that highlight their services, and you remember it because it's like listening to someone tell a story. Each ad finishes with, "And tell 'em Big Kenny sent ya." The results and feedback that Aim has had over the years because of Big Kenny are tremendous. They managed to take a rather boring business category, electrical, and bring it to life with a likeable and relatable character.

This is similar to what Precision Auto Body did with Rocco. Because of this strong character, listeners and customers pay attention and are always waiting to hear what Rocco will do next.

By creating a character to be the face of your brand, you can tell a story and add some personality to your business, especially if it's something that's normally boring for most people.

JINGLES

One of the most—if not *the* most—powerful and underrated branding tools is the musical image, or the jingle. Jingles get a bad rap because they are associated with cheesy synthesizer music from 1985, but stay with me here. Turn on a song that you loved in high school and you'll remember every word, every musical highlight, and even the way the singer sang it, and you can sing along exactly the way it is on the recording. Why is this? Because our brain takes in and processes music differently than the spoken word.

If you can sing all of those songs that you never meant to learn, what better way to brand your business into the long-term memory of your customers than by putting your message to music? If they can remember your tagline because they can't get your jingle out of their heads, how much more likely is it that you'll be remembered when they need what you sell?

My kids prove the effectiveness of musical images to me over and over. We usually have our local pop or news talk station on in the car when we're chauffeuring to dance, track, or piano, and that's the only time they hear the radio, so maybe 15–30 minutes a day. When I worked at the radio station, my kids would ask me, "Mom, who are your advertisers?" I would list a number of them, with little to no reaction because they didn't recognize the names. But whenever I named a business that had a jingle, all three of them would sing the jingle on the spot.

Just a couple of weeks ago, I mentioned that one of the kids was going to a birthday party at Ruckers Arcade, and my son sang, "When you're game for fun it's Ruckers. Ruckers when you're game for fun!"—the chorus of the Ruckers jingle.

When I said that I was going shopping to get a new mattress, my daughter (who is six years old) said, "Mom, why don't you go to Sleep Country? That's where you should go." Then she proceeded to sing, "Sleep Country Canada. Why buy a mattress anywhere else?"

And whenever I say I'm going to visit my friends Joe and Jennifer at Precision Auto Body, any one of the kids will sing, "Let Precision Auto Body work for you!"

These businesses are branded for *life* in the minds of my children and they aren't even old enough to make the purchase decisions. My oldest son is 13 and though I hate to think it, he will have his driver's license in three years, and though I *really* hate to think it, he may end up needing an auto body shop. Who do you think he is going to think of first and feel the best about?

Part of the reason that jingles have had a bad rap over the years is because some businesses produce them inexpensively, so they end up being low quality. People have been known to go through town selling canned jingles with "insert business name here" templates. The bad ones grate on listeners' nerves and they don't have a long shelf life. People quickly get sick of them and that's not good for your advertising. But when you do it right and hire a professional musical imaging producer who sources singers and musicians and composes your jingle just for you, it can show off your business' personality perfectly and stay relevant for many years. You might pay a little more up front, but like anything, you get what you pay for.

A typical jingle package should come with a full 60 second song, a full 30 second song, and various cuts with intros and extros (tagline sung at the end). And once you have your lyrics, you can use lines from the lyrics in your outdoor advertising and in print, and you can even have your jingle playing on your website and as your hold music on the phone. Talk about consistency in advertising!

When I first started working with Joe from Precision Auto Body, he had just bought the shop from the original owner after 30 years of business. Joe wanted to resurrect the well-known Precision jingle, so we tracked it down from the archives on eight-track! He's used it again for almost a decade and has no plans to stop. It now has a whole new generation of customers singing, "Let Precision Auto Body work for you!"

CELEBRITY ENDORSEMENTS

A celebrity endorsement is basically hiring a high-profile spokesperson. They can be anyone from actors to models to athletes, or even pop stars, businesspeople, politicians, or podcasters. National brands pay billions of dollars for celebrity endorsements, which are used to enhance brand value, create a positive feeling, provide a reason to buy, and differentiate companies from their competition. It is reported that about 25% of television commercials in the U.S. feature celebrities and the most iconic endorsements have contributed to pop culture over the last few decades.

Some of the most notable endorsements of our time include Michael Jordan's Nike Air Jordan campaign, Nicole Kidman for Chanel No. 5, and Britney Spears' endorsement of Pepsi. And who can forget Fabio promoting I Can't Believe It's Not Butter in the 90s? Or Priceline with the memorable voice of William Shatner? One of the most lucrative deals of all time went to George Foreman when he agreed to put his name to that famous fat-reducing grill. Foreman is said to be worth $250 million, with 90% stemming from the George Foreman Grill.

According to Experticity, celebrity endorsements actually carry 22 times more power of suggestion than a recommendation from an everyday customer. And an endorsement can work for small businesses for the same reasons it works for big brands. You don't need to hire Beyoncé or Tom Brady to see the benefits of a celebrity endorsement in your community. By hiring a local celebrity to speak for your brand, you can stand out in the market and have a positive effect on consumers.

But in order for an endorsement, especially one that is local, to be effective, the celebrity needs to be:

- **Credible**—the more credible the celebrity you choose, the bigger the impact they will have. The audience is most likely to respond when the celebrity has some connection to your industry.

- **Likeable**—the audience must be familiar with the celebrity, like them, and identify with them. If you choose someone who is well-known but unpopular, you could be creating negative associations with your brand.

- **Accessible and visible**—the celebrity needs to regularly appear in public. If it's a TV or radio personality, they should be accessible on their show by phone or messaging, on social media, and at station and client events.

- **Relatable**—the celebrity should have some tie-in with the product or service. If they are well-known as an athlete, you probably wouldn't use them to represent your renovation company.

You can harness the power of endorsements online as well. You can reach out to key influencers and thought-leaders in your business category and request that they showcase your products or company online (and they would need to clearly state that it is sponsored). You can also sponsor podcasts where the host endorses your product at the beginning or end of each episode. However, the only time online endorsements would make sense for a local business is if the podcast or blog or influencer has a large following in your local area (or you will be paying to reach people that are not in your trading area).

If you do choose to use a celebrity endorsement for your brand, it's a good idea to meet with them regularly and have them write their own script for talking about the business. The celebrity should have a good understanding of what you do and get regular updates about the message the business wants to send.

There are countless ways to be creative with an endorsement: you could have a picture of the celebrity in your store or office or have them host a couple of events with your customers, post pictures on social media, use your products in public, or appear in radio or TV ads, on your billboards and bus boards, and on your website.

If there is a good feeling associated with the celebrity—the same feeling that you want associated with your business—then a celebrity endorsement is a great way to build the brand image you desire. Think about the big endorsements I mentioned. Which ones do you think were the best fit with the story that brand wanted to tell?

TAGLINES AND SLOGANS

A tagline is the catch phrase or slogan you use in your advertising to sum up what you do. Like jingles, they offer a memorable way to communicate your message to your audience. And since they are not exclusively associated to audio, they can be the tie that binds your radio and TV ads with your billboards, website, and Facebook page. But for a tagline to be effective, it needs to be unique and meaningful.

If your current tagline is, "For all your [blank] needs," then this section is directed at you. "For all your rental needs."

"For all your banking needs." "For all your home audio needs." We see that all the time. It is so generic, you could literally insert any business name in there. If you can say your slogan, but replace your business name with a business from any category you can think of, then it's not a strong tagline. Instead, it should be specific to your business.

Some of the most recognizable taglines are:

- Just Do It. *Nike, 1988.*

- A diamond is forever. *DeBeers, 1948.*

- Good to the last drop. *Maxwell House, 1959.*

- Melts in your mouth, not in your hands. *M&M's, 1950s.*

- There are some things money can't buy. For everything else, there's MasterCard. *MasterCard, 1997.*

- Maybe she's born with it; maybe it's Maybelline. *L'Oréal, 1991.*

It's hard to believe some of these taglines have been around for so many years. And they're still just as relevant as ever.

It's not just national and international brands that can benefit from taglines. Small businesses can do a great job with slogans that have staying power, too. Some of ours include:

- We know our stuff. *Al Anderson's Source for Sports.*

- When you're game for fun. *Ruckers Arcade.*

- For special occasions, there's roses. For every day, there's Daisy's. *Daisy's Restaurant & Lounge.*

- Get fit before you run. *Brainsport.*

Effective taglines can last decades and get you into the long-term memory of your customers. But only if you do it right. Some companies spend huge amounts of money on terrible taglines that just don't work. The main culprits are ones that are confusing, complicated, vague, pretentious, or underwhelming. They can actually devalue a brand and create negative associations with your business. Consider these ones:

- Excellence through total quality. *Ames Rubber*.
- Ask why. *Enron*.
- What's your problem? *FileMaker Software*.
- Drive one. *Ford*.
- We want you to live. *Mobil*.
- Is that a Playtex under there? *Playtex*.

Trying to be too cute or forgetting to test out your taglines on your audience can be detrimental. Just for fun, let's look at a few slogans that went terribly wrong:

- A photographer: We shoot people and pets.
- Youth martial arts program: Building better kids one punch at a time.
- For a vacuum: Nothing sucks like an Electrolux.
- For a skincare line: Skin good enough to eat.
- Charmin paper: Why not enjoy the go?
- PBS Public Television: If PBS doesn't do it, who will?
- Carl's Jr. restaurants: If it doesn't get all over the place, it doesn't belong in your face.

Really, Carl's Jr.?

To help you avoid spending time and money developing a terrible tagline, here are some tips for creating one that will actually work for you:

- Keep it short and sweet (three to five words if possible)
- The more specific to your business, the better
- Include a key benefit
- Encapsulate the best thing about your company
- Differentiate yourself from your competition
- Don't be too cute!

THE FINER DETAILS

When it comes to advertising your company, it's easy to get caught up in all the exciting choices. Jingles, taglines, mascots, and endorsements are all excellent tactics to use in your advertising, but there are a few other details you will want to keep in mind through it all.

A STYLE YOU CAN STICK WITH

Becoming known for something means that your audience needs to hear your core message over and over again. Remember, it's all about salience *and* repetition. Therefore, it is important to develop a style and stick with it for a while. You want your brand and your message to become recognizable, so if you're sending out inconsistent messaging in many different styles, you don't give anyone the chance to register or internalize the message before they are hearing something different.

Before you start developing your advertising, decide on the things you plan to include every time you run a television commercial, or on every bus board you buy, or every time you buy an ad on Facebook. Keep the message consistent across all media, so that your audience recognizes it as being from the same brand. You will not include your entire radio script in an online banner ad, of course, but make sure there are core elements that stay consistent, so no matter where someone gets an impression of you, they will always get the same impression. That way, you're not reintroducing yourself and starting from scratch every time you talk to your audience. We'll look at a few tools to help you later in this chapter.

By building consistency, you can achieve familiarity with the audience so they think, "I know this company." Then, every time you add new information, they can focus on *that* rather than wondering, "Who is this?"

Planning an annual marketing campaign is like writing a novel. You have a lot that you need to get across to the reader, but you can't do it all in the first chapter. Your core message is the book cover: it's simple and summarizes what the book is about. Each chapter reveals a new element about your business, like new products, seasonal changes, or complementary services. Each chapter (or ad) only needs one main point because as soon as you try to cram more than one main thought into your ad, you'll lose your audience. Remember, "One thought, one spot."

STRONG CHOICE OF WORDS

Along with maintaining a consistent style across your ads, you'll need to find just the right words to spread your message. When you are purchasing advertising, copywriting will likely be included in your deal with the media or agency you are buying from. Instead of spending all your brain power coming up with your ad copy, let the professionals take care of it.

Copywriters have an amazing, complex, and important job to do, and are often undervalued for the art that they create day after day. They are asked to produce material that will connect with your ideal customer, convey the best of what your company has to offer, build a "relationship" with the audience, get attention, inform, and persuade…all in 10 lines or less!

What your message *says* is what will lead to the success of your advertising, so working with someone who knows what they are doing, and then trusting their recommendation (even if the ad actually sounds like an ad!) will bring you the best results. A well-written, persuasive message can be effective through almost any delivery vehicle.

The following are some of the attributes of good copywriting. If you've worked with copywriters before, consider what they have done for you. Have they been writing marketing poetry for you and you just didn't realize it?

A good ad:

- Focuses on the audience, rather than the business, by using words like you and your, not we, I, and us

- Builds intimacy with the audience
- Has wording inspired by literature and poetry, not newspaper articles and textbooks
- Is written based on what fits the strategy, not what fits your preferences
- Starts strong with a killer headline
- Doesn't talk down to your customers
- Includes a clear call to action (makes the sale)
- Doesn't use clichés or "ad-speak"
- Uses more verbs than adjectives ("action" words more than "describing" words)
- Talks in specifics rather than in generalities
- Is minimal and focuses on one thought at a time (one thought, one spot)
- Uses as few words as possible (while saying enough to get your message across)

Resist the urge to entertain yourself. The strategy comes first, so wrap the idea around the strategy, not the other way around.

The following are two ads that illustrate the difference between an interesting ad that paints a picture and uses creative language, and one that is completely focused on the details of the business. Which one leaves you with a better feeling about the company?

EXAMPLE #1

Sound effect: street ambience

Ten-year-old Sydney Barringer walks down the street after school on a Wednesday. He witnesses Mr. Reginald Johnson accidently dropping his wallet. Scooping it up, young Sydney realizes it's full of money; enough to buy Sydney a lot of comic books. But Sydney chases Mr. Johnson and hands him back his property. Mr. Johnson is exuberantly thankful to the young man, as this money was to pay his mortgage. This is a Pete's Auto Body moment. Pete teaches his people that quality means doing it right when no one else is looking. Honesty lives at Pete's, on Avenue P South.[2]

EXAMPLE #2

Pete's Auto Body is a one stop shop for all your car repair needs. The Pete's team are proud to have the city's most revolutionary paint booth! It's one of the first of its kind in the city. It will give your vehicle a factory finish or better. For 20 years, the Pete's Auto Body team have been bringing their customers the ultimate in service and quality finishing. Pete's is an insurance accredited auto body shop and the leader in automobile paint technique. Visit Pete's Auto Body. 10-09 Avenue P South.[3]

Which one paints a picture and focuses on benefits for the customer? Which one stands out from the competitors? People often end up with ads that are like example #2 because they are easier to write and more common. But #1 applies elements that make up an excellent ad and will be more memorable and effective.

PLANNING TOOLS

Keeping your ads meaningful and consistent over time can be a challenge when you have so many other parts of your business to worry about. As new ideas and opportunities come up, it can be easy to forget the details of your current campaign strategy and unintentionally shift the focus of your messages.

To help you out, I've included two tools that you can use to track your ads and ensure the best chance of keeping them consistent. They'll help you as you build your creative strategy so that you don't have to keep reinventing the wheel.

To illustrate both tools, we'll use the Awl Shoppe, our quality luggage store, as an example. Luggage is still their primary focus, but they also have a shoe and repair department, and over the years have expanded their offering into travel accessories and a small selection of other leather goods.

CREATIVE MANUAL

The creative manual is the hard cover of your book. It's the title page on the front, and the synopsis on the back. This is a list of the things that will "bookend" your messaging to help your ads stay consistent throughout the campaign, so you don't lose your focus and veer off course or try to change things the second you grow bored.

To develop your creative manual, make a point form list of things you will always include or keep in mind for any ad created in this campaign. It will be important that your media copywriters and online content developers stick to the creative manual so your messaging is consistent across the board. It can even help you when it's time to develop your next campaign and keep track of what you've done before.

In the case of the Awl Shoppe, their creative manual (for radio) looked like this:

- Always start with, "Taking a trip? Start at the Awl Shoppe."
- Include, "From entry level nylon to high-end amazing," in the body.
- Always end with, "Take a trip—to the Awl Shoppe."
- Locator: North of Earl's on 2nd Avenue.
- Music: Sunday Cruise
- Voice: Shauna

Although these are the points applied specifically to radio commercials, you would still keep these elements in mind when creating billboards, print ads, TV ads, or online posts. You want to keep everything as consistent as possible across all your media. However, you would have different variations of the manual for each of the delivery vehicles. For example, your TV ad would need fewer words as the visuals help tell the story, and in print, you'd want to include a headline, striking image, and call to action as well. The Awl Shoppe's creative manual applied to a magazine ad would look like this:[4]

- Headline/call to action: "Taking a trip? Start at the Awl Shoppe."
- Image of luggage/vacation

- Body text: "Entry level nylon to high-end amazing."
- Font: Tahoma
- Color pallette: Olive, suede, saffron
- Awl Shoppe logo
- Contact information: Address, phone number and website

CREATIVE CALENDAR

If the creative manual is the hard cover of the book, the creative calendar makes up the chapters. Figure out what you want your audience to have heard about you by the end of this year. Start by making a point-form list of all of the things you'd like them to know. For the Awl Shoppe, it was:

- We repair shoes, boots, and bags.
- We have a travel accessory section.
- We have entry-level to high-end luggage.
- We have holiday stocking stuffers suitable for almost everyone.
- We carry locally made slippers and mittens.

Then take a calendar and plot in what you should be talking about as each season comes; in effect, telling your story one chapter at a time. For example:

- **January–February**—warm holidays; luggage focus
- **March**—early spring; time to pull your spring and summer footwear out of storage and get it repaired and ready for the season

- **April–mid-May**—the importance of having good luggage
- **Mid-May–June**—promote luggage as a graduation gift idea
- **July**—Europe travel; travel accessories (they actually have quick-dry undies that you can wash daily and wear every day of your trip—talk about packing light!)
- **August**—the importance of having good luggage
- **September**—time to pull out your winter boots from storage and have them repaired before the snow comes
- **October–November**—warm holidays; luggage focus
- **November–December**—Christmas gift ideas; stocking stuffers, slippers, etc.

By developing a creative calendar and making sure your copywriter works from it, you avoid getting to the middle of a season and saying, "Oh shoot, we should've been talking about this in our advertising," or getting into October while still running the "Summer's here" ad!

You should also apply your creative calendar to your social media activity. There are useful social media management tools available online that allow you to plan your posts so they happen automatically on a pre-set schedule (rather than throwing random posts up when you have three minutes to yourself in the washroom! Admit it—you've done it!)

WHEN IS IT TIME TO REFRESH?

Business owners have the tendency to get bored and want to change their messaging *way* too early in a campaign. Most advertisers are going to get tired of their own commercials well before anybody else has even started to notice them. Keep in mind that you are very close to your advertising. You planned it, you're proud of it (and nervous about it), and you feel like you're putting yourself out there in a big, vulnerable way. So naturally you notice it more; you hear the ads every time they play on the radio and you watch for your billboard when you're driving downtown. But your ads are not as salient to your audience as they are to you. Most of your potential customers are going to just start noticing your ads when you're already sick of them and ready to change it up. Be patient. ***Branding is a marathon, not a sprint.***

If you change your style every six weeks, you are sending a mixed message to the market. Moreover, you'll be reintroducing and re-explaining yourself all over again every time. You want people to become familiar with your message, to be able to sing your jingle, and to know your tagline before you consider changing your ads. The key lines of your message need to become known, like brandable bits that bounce around in the mind of your customer and come to the surface when they need what you sell.

A potential customer needs to be exposed to your message at least three times before they will even notice it or pay attention to it. (Some say six, seven, or even 10 times!) And as we know, your advertising is first building visibility, then credibility, and finally profitability. So, remember that profitability doesn't happen right away. You need to be willing to stay the course and focus on the horizon. Think long-term about your ads.

Having said all of this, though, eventually you'll need to freshen things up. The creative manual is specifically for the style and wording of your messaging, so it will eventually change when it is time to freshen up the campaign. While your manual can change, your core values and message should be constant. New ads don't need to reinvent the wheel; they just need to deliver the old in a new and different way.

A local home renovations company I know of had been around and well-known for over three decades. Due to some changes in their company and its affiliates, they needed to change their name. As they were planning to roll out the name change, their marketing department decided they only wanted to advertise the change for three months, then exclusively start using the new name. This company was not a client of mine, so I wasn't close to it, but about eight months after the name changed, I finally realized that this new renovation company I'd been hearing about was actually that old company!

They'd been branding the old name for 30 years in this city, so they should have been explaining the name change for a lot longer than just three months to make sure that the good brand image they'd built was transferred over to the new name. "You know us, you trust us, we've just changed the name—the quality is still the same." By jumping ship too early, they lost a lot of the brand equity that they'd built over so many years. To avoid making this mistake, your message should stay consistent for a length of time that is proportionate to what you're trying to accomplish or how long you've built up a different message in the market.

Some of the advertisers that have been very successful have kept the same style for one, two, or even three or more years. If you are consistently getting plenty of new customers and seeing a consistent growth in sales, then your branding message is doing its job—there's no need to change it just yet.

Reaction vs. results

Since ads can become personal, most business owners get nervous about and sensitive to their customers' and friends' reactions. Most of the time, you're probably *only* hearing from the people close to you: friends, family, staff, and maybe a few regular customers. This can be really encouraging because you start to think, "Oh good, people are seeing my ads."

However, your perspective is probably a bit skewed because how many customers really come into your store and say, "I came to shop here today because of the charming and effective TV commercial I saw"? I'm guessing none. Customers don't have any vested interest in telling you that, or for that matter even remembering exactly where they heard about you. So even though it's nice and reassuring to get some reaction, that will soon fade as the novelty wears off. And that's okay. The reaction is not really what we're looking for with our ads.

What we are waiting for is the results. And those come later—from the people you don't know, who won't tell you they saw your ad, but who will start opening their wallets. If you jump ship as soon as the initial reaction wears off, you are selling yourself short. Once you see results coming in, watch the growth of your sales. If they are growing at a consistent rate, your message is still getting through. And on top of that, keep in mind that there are always new people entering your potential customer pool who weren't there last year—new people moving into the city, people having babies who didn't need baby clothes a year ago, people deciding that they want to get in shape who were couch potatoes last year. They may have heard your ad for the last year, but didn't need the fitness clothing you are selling until right now, so your message (though you may be bored of it) is brand new to them right now!

As David Ogilvy taught, "You are advertising to a parade, not a standing army." Your audience is always on the move; in and out of different life stages and buying cycles. So, that same ad that sold cross country skis to the young couple two years ago will likely sell cross country skis to a different couple this year.[5]

When you are developing the creative style of your messages, do not be tempted to choose a style just to get a reaction or to entertain yourself or your audience. It is more important to get results. The ads that persuade people to buy may not always be the most entertaining, but they will prove themselves over time as your customer base increases and your business grows.

• • •

When it comes to developing your message, there are tons of options to choose from. Whether you opt for a catchy jingle or a cute mascot, or you simply stick with excellent copy that connects with your audience, your ads will benefit most from consistency and long-term thinking. Remember, we are not playing a three-month game; advertising and branding can take time to build. In fact, most brands advertise for the entire lifetime of their business because with each campaign they run, they see higher and higher rates of return and more and more growth. If you want that to be you, focus on keeping your messaging consistent within your chosen media and commit to long-term branding.

But of course, this isn't all that marketing is. In Chapter 5, we'll look at the advertising toolbox and explore the different kinds of media you can use to reach your audience. Before we get there, though, think about what you've been doing with your advertisements so far and the ways you can improve your message.

HOMEWORK

1. What were the last three messages you put into the market?

2. Do those messages all contribute to the same idea or do they introduce different ideas?

3. Do your messages clearly state to the audience why you exist?

4. Do they make clear the *benefit* to your customers or just the details about your business? ie. what's in it for your audience to do business with you?

5. Do your commercials aim to persuade, inform, or simply entertain your audience?

CHAPTER 5

The Advertising Toolbox

"Advertising is criticized on the grounds that it can manipulate consumers to follow the will of the advertiser...evidence denies this ability. Instead...advertising, to be successful, must understand or anticipate basic human needs and wants, and interpret available goods and services in terms of their want-satisfying abilities. This is the very opposite of manipulation."

—David Ogilvy

Advertising gets a bad rap. People unfairly paint it with a big negative brush because there have been so many hard-selling, cliché-yelling, dishonest, gimmicky ad campaigns over the years. But not all advertising falls under that umbrella.

We celebrate and hail entrepreneurs who have risked it all to bring us new ideas, new products or new services. The CEOs of startups are pop culture's new heroes, but then we say that they shouldn't promote their stuff? Communicating what they can do for us is the only way they will grow and succeed. Some will achieve viral success through PR and the buzz they create, but not all businesses who are worthy of our money will get that kind of press. If they don't send us a message somehow, nobody will know how much value they could add to our lives.

When people say, "Traditional advertising is dead," they really mean we don't want to be insulted with a self-serving ad message. But if you're a good company who can actually benefit me, of course I want you to tell me about it!

As a small business owner, it is so difficult to decide where to focus your messaging and invest your limited (and hard-earned!) advertising dollars. If you're in retail, you no doubt get emails, phone calls, and stop-ins every week from people trying to sell you some form of advertising. Every advertising rep says that they have the right product to reach your customers and grow your business, and many of them really could achieve that for you.

But where it becomes tricky is that not all advertising vehicles are meant to serve the same purpose and achieve the same kind of results for advertisers. They are often compared as if they are—they are all painted with the same brush—so results are disappointing because businesses haven't chosen the right advertising vehicles to achieve the objectives they've set. On top of that, not all people who can sell you advertising in media or online actually understand branding or how to use their products effectively to grow your business. And, of course, there are always sales reps who are looking for a quick sale instead of a long-term partnership that will benefit both your business and theirs.

In this chapter, we will go through the hierarchy of advertising and I'll explain what each of the options is meant to achieve and which business objectives they are suited for. We'll start by looking at three fundamental concepts of advertising before we get into your options.

THREE FUNDAMENTAL CONCEPTS

There are three concepts that we need to explore and understand before we get into the advertising toolbox. These are instrumental and form the basis for deciding which advertising tools to reach for. They are CCF, sight versus sound, and the role of online marketing.

CCF: CONSISTENCY, CREATIVITY, FREQUENCY

Business owners are often discouraged and overwhelmed because most advertising advice tells them they need to figure out how to be in front of the perfect customer *exactly* when they're most motivated to make a purchase. How does one do that? From my perspective, unless you have a functioning crystal ball, you can't predict exactly when they'll need you. So, unless you can get right inside their minds, you'll have to come up with something else. A more effective way to get on your customers' shopping lists is to become a household name and maintain that status by sending constant reminders to your market so they know about you *before* they need you.

The most important foundation you will need to build into your advertising is a campaign that achieves CCF: Consistency, Creativity, and Frequency. The ultimate goal in marketing should be to become a household name among your target audience and that means you have to consistently and creatively send your message to your customers at a frequency that keeps you top-of-mind. You want to be thought of with a good feeling when the need for what you offer arises. Yes, I said they need to think of you *when the need arises*, but in order for that to happen, you need to have convinced your audience of your worth *before* they are ready to make a purchase decision.

CONSISTENCY

Maintain a presence in the minds of your audience on a year-round basis so they think of you first and feel the best about you when they need what you sell. This means choosing an audience and sticking to it, rather than bouncing all over the place. When you pick an audience and own them, you can clearly and efficiently direct your messaging to them.

If you have a small budget and are targeting narrowly (through Facebook targeted ads, for example), you would advertise to your niche markets. But when you're looking at a media audience, you have to go broader. Literally pick a chunk of the market—whether that's a single neighborhood that you blanket with billboards or a single radio station's listening audience—and then own that group of people 52 weeks of the year. Within any mass media audience group, there will be more than enough people who are your potential customers or who know your potential customers, so pick something you feel good about and commit to it.

When you can manage to *consistently* advertise to just that one market, you will stay on their mind. Because you won't take weeks or months off from your advertising, your message is always there for them to hear or see. That's great, but it's only part of the puzzle.

CREATIVITY

The next job is to create a message that is compelling enough that it catches your audience's attention. It has to clearly define the benefit your company offers in an interesting way.

In the last chapter, we looked at elements of ads, like jingles, mascots, and slogans, that can make your ad campaign and brand memorable. Being clear in your messaging, and being *interesting* in the style in which you deliver it will be what makes your ads salient. This means more people are going to recognize your brand and want to shop at your store.

By being memorable, you are enabling your audience to hear your message and keep it in mind, despite all the other brand messages they receive all day.

FREQUENCY

Remember that you want to get into the long-term memory of your customers. That's where the final piece of the CCF puzzle—frequency—comes in. Even though you are consistently advertising with a creative message, you still have to make sure your audience hears about you *often enough* to keep you top-of-mind.

An ideal frequency would be that your potential customer hears your ad three times every seven-nights' sleep for *at least a year* before you will become branded in their mind (with an average impact commercial). Why do we talk about sleep here? Because sleep is the great eraser of advertising.[1] Every night when we go to sleep, our brain erases the majority of the clutter that it was bombarded with in the day, including the advertising. It has to, or we would go crazy. So, what sticks and gets into long-term memory? Only those things that we hear many times, week-in and week-out.

When you crave a burger and fries, what business comes to mind?

When you need flowers for your mom on Mother's Day, where would you go?

When you have to pick up a bottle of wine, is there a store you'd think of immediately? And would you share that wine with me?

You likely have a business in your town that you'd think of when you need these things. And it's not because they timed their ad placement specifically for when you were most motivated to buy. You thought of them first because of the frequency with which you hear and see their message. You drive by their store, read their billboards, hear their radio commercials, hear about them from your friends, or see social media posts from them. Those impressions were all made on you before the moment you made the purchase decision. And they have all worked together to make sure that those businesses are at the top of your shopping list.

Now sometimes a well-timed ad *can* tip the scale and motivate you to act, like if it's 11:30 at night and you're *really hungry* and you happen to see an Instagram post of a juicy burger and fries from Joe's Burger Joint, that may have you saying "ohmygodthatsoundsamazingrightnowimsohungry!" But more than likely, your past experiences with Joe's (friends talking about it, street signage, media ads) have added to your instant recognition of the promise the Instagram post holds and your conviction to put on some pants and drive down there right now.

Usually when an advertiser tries a campaign and it doesn't work, one or more of the elements of Clarity, Creativity, and Frequency (CCF) is missing from their strategy. We will explore CCF in greater detail in Chapter 6, but keep these in mind as we go through the strengths and appropriate uses of each of your options, because as you make your advertising decisions, you'll measure each choice against how well they achieve CCF.

SIGHT VS. SOUND

Another fundamental of advertising that applies to the type of media you choose for your messaging is sight versus sound. Each plays a different role in the impact of commercials. While sight works to visualize a product or service, sound is intrusive and reaches your brain differently.

How often have you read the same paragraph over and over but have no idea what you just read? How often have you read the same paragraph over and over but have no idea what you just read? (haha gotcha!) It's possible (and actually very common) to see something but not register it in your mind. The way your brain processes the things you see is very different than how it processes what you hear.

When you were a kid in school and you weren't paying attention, did your teacher ever call your name and say, "What did I just say?" and you could repeat what she had said verbatim? That's common because our minds take in sound even when we aren't actively listening. Just yesterday, my 10-year-old son was playing his 3DS in the back seat of the car as we were driving to piano lessons. The radio was playing in the background as the rest of us were chatting. The announcer posed a question to the listeners and my son, out of nowhere, looked up from his video game and shouted out an answer. Then, he said, "Weird—I wasn't even listening to that!"

It is possible, and probable, that you will not notice or recall many of the ads in the magazine or paper you read. Readers of a newspaper or magazine will most likely notice an ad in the publication only if they are actively in the market for what is being advertised.[2] So, the print advertiser pays to reach the whole reading audience, but only actually makes an impact on the people who were actively looking for the products advertised.

We don't consciously listen to every radio commercial that is played, but our brains register the information and an impression is made on us even before we're in the market. We can't help but know about the businesses who speak to us every day over the airwaves. So, when you advertise on radio and TV, you are making impressions on those who are in the market now *and* those who will be in the market in the future. Buying a medium that allows you to make impressions on both those groups is, effectively, branding your business.

In fact, in 1971, the Federal Communications Commission placed a complete ban on all radio and TV advertising for cigarette and tobacco companies in the US because they were deemed too effective in promoting the use of tobacco. However, they continued to allow advertising for these products in newspapers, magazines, and billboards. Because sound is so much more persuasive than sight in advertising, they didn't restrict billboard advertising until almost 30 years later. The ban is still in effect today, but anyone who was around before 1971 can still recall the jingles of some of the big cigarette companies.

Sight and sound in advertising is a bigger deal than most people think. All advertising can make impressions, but sound makes an emotional connection. Sound can make you *feel* a certain way (think about how you feel when you hear your favorite song from high school or select your iPod workout mix to pump you up when you are heading out for a run). Ads with sight make an impression, but ads with sound create an emotion. How do you want your audience to *feel*?

When it comes to advertising, adding media that includes sound will be much more effective for your branding than sticking with sight-only options. You will make lasting impressions on more people and get into long-term memory faster with sound, especially when you use memorable creative messaging.

ONLINE PRESENCE: THE NEW SHINY TOY

Over the last decade, the world has shifted its focus and an unimaginably huge opportunity to communicate globally has emerged. The Internet has brought us connectivity, convenience, and a whole new set of opportunities that we couldn't have dreamed of 50 years ago. Because of all the new platforms on which we can reach people, companies have naturally turned to the Internet to reach their customers, and in turn, customers have come to expect their favorite stores and brands to be online when they want to find them. An online presence has become fundamental to advertising success.

If you are in business today, it is crucial to have some sort of presence online. If someone hears about you and can't find you on the Internet for more information, you have likely lost that prospect. So, having a website is actually a really important brand element.

However, there is a big—*huge*—misperception out there that online advertising can and should replace traditional advertising. In reality, online advertising should be considered a *complement* to traditional advertising, rather than a substitute. Because of all the new online adventures that await advertisers and because everyone has been on a massive learning curve on the subject, the majority of articles, books, and resources about advertising lately have focused on online options.

As with anything new, it takes a while to figure things out. In the last five years, the all-encompassing word "online" has brought fear and confusion to business owners everywhere. Where they once understood the concept of advertising, they are now becoming confused and overwhelmed with all the options. So, they've handed their advertising budgets over to individuals and agencies who offer to manage their online presence without understanding for themselves what they should be doing or what they can expect for their money.

Because the options and activities and rules of engagement online are constantly changing, there is an endless flurry of advice and information overload. Though most articles and reports are overly focused on the online portion of your advertising plan, if you look closely, the ones written by some of the most credible authors will point out that online marketing is meant to be part of a bigger plan, and not enough if done as a stand-alone tactic.

Online can be a very good complement and accelerator to the other advertising you are doing. Your media advertising now has somewhere to send customers to get information and engage with you before committing to coming to your store. To complement that, having an online presence can enhance the results you are getting offline and create more of a tribe feeling than traditional advertising and branding alone.

Our Italian friend, Rocco, who represents Precision Auto Body on the radio, was featured in an ad that had to do with Facebook, or "Bookface" as Rocco calls it. He was trying to figure out how to be on the Bookface, and how to post a car on a wall. We started running the ad and guess what happened? Joe started getting 50 new Facebook followers a day on the Precision Auto Body page! Making those connections on social media allowed Precision to build deeper relationships with more of their clients because they could now interact with them using two-way communication on social media. When they want to make an announcement to their followers, those followers can share, comment on, and ask questions about that new piece of information. They can build a *community* around their business and get even more buy-in from their clients.

Online marketing doesn't have to be scary. It can actually be hugely beneficial to your brand to have an online presence, but just remember not to assume that your focus should be only online if you want to build your customer base. Think of online options as just another set of tools in your toolbox of ways to reach your customers. There are platforms that can help you manage your social media on your own, or you can surely find some very good online marketing agencies in your area who can help you narrow down a plan and implement it for you. Just remember that you never have to use every single tool in the box for every project.

Increasingly, marketing agencies understand the role that online tools should play as a part of your overall marketing plan—in combination with your outside media. You'll be best served by firms that understand how to effectively balance online and offline tools.

IT'S MEASURABLE

Advertisers have been excited about online advertising because they finally have something they can easily measure. You can see how many people clicked on an ad, for how many seconds someone watched a video, how many people visited a website, how much time is spent on each page, and how many likes and re-tweets and follows you have. Advertisers like those numbers because they don't get that kind of data from traditional media advertising.

The problem is, advertisers tend to focus on the wrong things when analyzing their online marketing success. For example, they judge their results by how many likes they get on a post. But likes are a passive gesture, like a nod two acquaintances may share as they pass each other on the street. It's an acknowledgement, but little more. It's easy to get caught up in the popularity contest of likes, but how many likes would you need to result in a true positive impact on your business? It doesn't matter if it's trackable when it's not actually selling your product. In Chapter 7, we'll talk about how to set goals to measure outcomes that matter.

SHOULD I GO ALL-IN ONLINE?

Traditional mass media can be frustrating for advertisers—it's harder to directly measure the effects of traditional advertising in newspapers and on TV and radio, etc. But, a good way to understand their impact is to measure what happens when they are removed from the equation.

In 2010, Pepsi cancelled all TV and Super Bowl advertising, and moved their money online to run the "Pepsi Refresh Project," which was a social media campaign. This campaign cost them somewhere between $50 and 100 million. With all that money, they got 3.5 million Facebook "likes," while at the same time, they experienced a 5% loss in market share representing a loss of over $350 million dollars, from which, as of the time of this writing, they have not recovered. They also dropped from second-bestselling soft drink in the world to third. *The LA Times* called the Pepsi campaign "a stunning fall from grace." Examples like this are reported more and more frequently as the shiny new toy that is social media marketing is being tested for longer periods.

That's not to say, though, that social media marketing is bad. In many cases, businesses with an effective social media presence don't need anything else to thrive. In other cases, it's a combination of both online and traditional that make up an effective campaign.

The conventional wisdom of today says that nobody reads the paper, listens to the radio, or watches TV anymore. But conventional wisdom is just that—conventional, convenient. That does not make it true. Anyone can Google the viewership and listenership numbers and see that these media are still delivering huge audiences all over the world. People of *all ages* (not just Baby Boomers, as some people think) still live out in the real world and see billboards, listen to the radio, and watch TV. But many of those same people who are exposed to these media every day seem to think that nobody else is seeing and hearing the same things they are.

Commercial television, print, and radio are called mass media because they reach the masses, and are *still* reaching the masses. Yes, the daily paper will soon be history, but outdoor, TV, and radio are still just as powerful a force as they have ever been and many print publications are just as popular as ever.

When advertisers have aggressive growth goals, they cannot ignore mass media. Why? It goes back to casting a bigger net if you want to catch more fish. There is some targetability within mass media (certain genres apply to different demographics), but you will still reach *way* more people than just your perfect customer. And that's a good thing. Because, again, nobody makes decisions in a vacuum. You will reach a whole bunch of potential customers, but you will *also* reach their influencers. If you had the chance to talk to 75,000 people about your business, even if they weren't all your perfect target, wouldn't you take it?

Because advertisers are starting to realize that dropping mass media completely will have an adverse effect on their businesses, new research is being conducted right now on the effectiveness of radio in Canada, the United States, and Great Britain. Some of it is even funded by the corporations who are purchasing all of the advertising on the media— they know they need it, but they need to show their shareholders why they are fighting the new "conventional wisdom." The radioGAUGE Canada study has repeatedly shown that adding radio to a big brand's media mix still has a huge impact;[3] radio increases ad recall of a brand by 149% and it is 22% more likely to drive consideration. Moreover, radio boosts brand browsing online by 52%![4]

It is interesting to note that in the last few years, many of the biggest spenders on radio and TV advertising in the United States were *all online businesses*. Travel websites are a great example of how being online alone is not always enough. Together, these sites spent $624 million on TV advertising in 2014. Trivago was the 7th biggest spender on TV and radio *of any brand in the United States*, spending a whopping $108 million to drive traffic to their website. Expedia was close behind when it spent $105 million. These companies only exist online and could not grow their businesses enough by advertising there! How do our local brick-and-mortar businesses expect to achieve what these huge online companies can't?

It is true that in the next five years, the money spent on online advertising will surpass that of TV advertising in the

US, but my prediction is that things will come back around and that traditional media will continue to adapt how they deliver their content in order to stay relevant to audiences. More big brands will realize that their brand recognition is decreasing and that social media "likes" don't equal revenue.

Although big brands continue to announce their move toward all online marketing, we can't ignore the fact that they would not be internationally recognized brands they are today without old media. They wouldn't see the success that they are seeing online if their TV, billboard, magazine, and radio ads hadn't turned them into household names. Without impressions from mass media, when you see a Coca-Cola ad online, all the emotions that you've associated with that brand would not exist. How many big consumer brands have been built online alone? Any success stories to date? [...crickets...]

BUT IT'S STILL ADVERTISING

The Internet is the shiny new toy, but it's still advertising. A podcast sponsorship is still an ad, just like a TV commercial is. Whether the message makes an impact on a consumer through a new platform or a traditional one will ultimately depend on its relevance to the viewer's life. As we covered earlier in this book, advertising is welcome if the product it's promoting adds value through an honest message and offering, no matter the format.

As the advertising industry grows and changes, we focus on telling a compelling story and reaching an audience consistently. It's not about hard-sell tactics, but about connecting with customers. The new world of online advertising should be measured and judged just as thoroughly as the old-school stuff. Online channels are simply new delivery vehicles of the same messages.

THE TOOLBOX

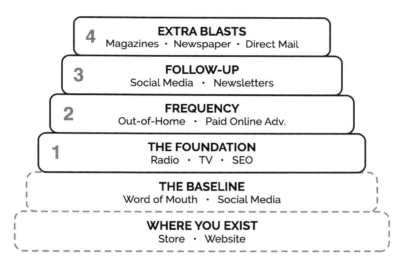

4 **EXTRA BLASTS**
Magazines · Newspaper · Direct Mail

3 **FOLLOW-UP**
Social Media · Newsletters

2 **FREQUENCY**
Out-of-Home · Paid Online Adv.

1 **THE FOUNDATION**
Radio · TV · SEO

THE BASELINE
Word of Mouth · Social Media

WHERE YOU EXIST
Store · Website

Having examined some fundamentals of advertising, we now turn to the Advertising Toolbox. This is an explanation and summary of all the most common options for advertising media. It is up to you to decide which ones work for you and for your objectives. That being said, this toolbox is designed to help you make those decisions.

We will start with the tools that establish your branding foundation at the bottom of the pyramid and work our way up through to the ones that will add interest and periodic extra blasts to your voice in the market. You'll notice that a couple of the tools appear in more than one layer of advertising. This is because these ones can play more than one role.

While you're reading through the options, determine where you are in your business and what you need out of your advertising. If you have a well-established brand in the market and are constantly booked up a month in advance, you may not need to do anything at the baseline branding level and you can skip to features and stories. Basically, I'm giving you the tools you need to choose your own adventure here.

For a small local business, I rarely recommend a media mix. Very few businesses would have a big enough budget to do more than one or two things well, so by no means should you consider doing *all* the things on the list at the same time!

WHERE YOU EXIST

Where you exist is the basis of your advertising. If you are a brick and mortar business, the two places you exist are your physical location (store, clinic, etc.) and your website. If you are online-only you just have one place. The places you exist should be where you direct all your advertising traffic. For a brick and mortar business, your ads should point your customers to your street address and your website.

Many people think of their website as online advertising, but it isn't. It doesn't *reach people* with your message. Instead, it sits and waits for people to visit and requires messaging to direct traffic to it. Having a website without sending people to it is like putting up a billboard in the middle of a field. It looks great, but nobody knows to go see it.

Your store

Your physical location advertises itself to the people who walk or drive by—the more traffic your location gets, the more visibility you have and the less advertising you will need. Conversely, the more out of the way your location is, the more advertising you will require to bring people to you.

If your business is on a high-traffic street, you should be taking as much advantage of that drive-by traffic as possible. Window signage and displays and easy-to-read signs on your building are all ways to the draw attention of those who pass by. Black and fluorescent neon signs are great (and versatile) to catch drivers' attention and sandwich boards on the sidewalk are great for walk-by traffic. A hot tub store in the north end of our city has had a gigantic blow-up rubber ducky on their roof for years. Use your physical signage to draw a (figurative) big red arrow above your business and capture the eyes of the thousands of people driving and walking past every day.

Your website

Your website is the other place where you exist. It is where people go to find out more about your offering and get your phone number, hours, and location. Once someone has heard about you from your ads or through friends and family, their next step is usually to go to your website before deciding if they will do business with you. In some cases, of course, shoppers can make a purchase right on your site.

If you have nothing else online, the basic requirement these days is to have a functional website. If somebody is considering buying from you, there is a good chance they will look for you online first. If they can't find any trace of you, you become almost irrelevant and cease to be a consideration in their purchase decision. If you don't have a website, you are as good as the faceless, nameless handyman you tried to hire from the online classifieds... who never showed up.

Developing a website can seem like a huge task but it doesn't have to be. No need for fancy scrolling animations or dozens of pages. At minimum, it should have:

- Your phone number, address and directions (preferably easy to find on the main page)
- An explanation of what your company does (the products or services you provide)
- A list of your hours of operation
- A form where they can send you a message

It needs to be mobile optimized as well. This means that it is easy to view on a mobile device and is properly formatted for that device as well. Nearly all new sites are built that way, but if you have an old site that is not mobile-friendly, get it updated as soon as possible. More and more of the time people spend online is on their mobile devices (smart phones, tablets, etc.) rather than desktop or laptop computers. Plus, Google penalizes you in search results if your site is not mobile optimized.

On top of the bare minimum, your website should also feature a call to action, encouraging your customer to take the next step. Whether that's buying online or coming into your store or signing up for your newsletter, you need to make sure you tell your customers what you want them to do next.

Keeping the site updated is another key to a successful online presence. If your website was last updated in June 2013, or it features a calendar of events from last season, your customers will dismiss the rest of the content. Although you should be updating it regularly, if you don't expect to keep up with it, avoid including time-specific items like events calendars or news feeds.

Your advertising is meant to persuade, and your website is meant to inform. So, once they hear the "why" from your ads, your customers will go to your website for the "what." You have unlimited opportunity on your website to educate customers on what you offer, who your staff is, why you started the business, and what brands you carry. The amount of content you want to include is up to you, and as long as you have the basics I've listed, the rest is a bonus. The more interesting and useful your content is, the more time visitors will spend with your site and the better they will get to know your business.

In any case, your website should be clean, professional, and easy to navigate. Remember, visiting your site is a step toward doing business with you, so it needs to make a good impression.

E-COMMERCE

For some businesses, it makes sense to have the option of buying products on your website. This takes your website and the costs and work associated with it to a whole new level. Before jumping on the bandwagon and implementing an e-commerce element to your website, consider the following:

- Is there a real opportunity to expand your market beyond your immediate trading area? Selling online would open up the option of gaining customers from a wider market who want your products shipped to them. Have you tapped out the potential in your immediate trading area or is there still room to grow with in-person sales?

- Is there enough of a selling opportunity to justify hiring someone to fill, pack, and ship online orders and deal with returns and out-of-town customers? And to continually update each individual product and price on your website? I have had clients who have cancelled their online store after realizing it was no fun selecting, wrapping, and shipping items all week long—and that it didn't pay for itself in sales.

- If you add e-commerce to your website, you will have to invest in advertising to let people know that you're open for business online.

You are not Amazon. I know you're shocked to hear this, but it's true. As soon as you move into online selling, your competition playing field gets that big. You are no longer just competing with the other businesses in your category in your city, but also Amazon and a whole host of other national and international retailers. Amazon will always have more commodity products for cheaper, but if you have a unique product line or something that is sought after and hard to find on huge online shopping sites, you can do very well with online sales.

For example, there is an apparel shop here in our city that makes clothing with designs highlighting both our local culture and the province as a whole. This is something that makes sense to offer for sale on their website because people from all over the province shop the online store and expats who are proud of where they came from order when they can't visit in person. And there are other local retailers who do really well with their online sales even to the local market simply because enough people would rather have things delivered than go out shopping, and their purchases are easier to return than it would be with Amazon, because the store is right in town.

Most of you, my readers, are in business primarily to serve your local customers. Adding an online shopping element makes sense only if the amount of time and energy it requires will be justified in the profit from that endeavor. But if it will take away from the attention you give your "lowest hanging fruit"—your walk-in customers—it could be detrimental.

Local businesses are often fearful that online giants like Amazon and eBay will kill their business, but you do have an advantage over these online retailers. And that is that people can come in to your store and physically see, touch, and try your products. But more importantly, customers can experience exceptional service, have their questions answered, and get real, in-person support. If you do a good job in your store, then you can hold your own against the drones who are picking and shipping parcels from a warehouse. I can order a pair of running shoes online, but Brainsport can measure my feet, watch the way I walk and run, fit shoes to my needs, include me in their weekly running club and yearly fundraiser marathon, and tell me which are the best running trails around our riverbank.

Eb's Source for Adventure shared a surprising effect of launching an e-commerce website. Though they have few people actually order products through the site, their in-store sales went up by 20% when the new site launched. Why do you think that is? It's because now every one of their products *and* their prices are listed on their website. People can now browse online and know that the store has what they're looking for and how much they will be paying; they can comparison shop ahead of time. Purchase decisions can be made before they ever walk into the store and then the transaction is as simple as coming in and saying, "I want this item that you have listed at this price."

So, remember, if you have nothing else going on online at all, have a website. Figure out what you would like the customer to use your website for, and tailor it to accomplish that. Then use your messaging to invite visitors to it. You don't have to feature an e-commerce option, and you don't have to make it fancy either. What you do need, though, is to have a way for people to find out more about you before coming to see you.

THE BASELINE

Advertising comes in many forms. Just like where you exist (online and off) provides a small amount of advertising for your business, your baseline is the bare minimum advertising you get just from existing and putting your name out in the world. It includes both word of mouth and social media communication.

WORD OF MOUTH

If I had a dollar for every time a business owner said to me, "To be honest with you, word of mouth is my number one form of advertising," I'd be writing this book from a private beach in Hawaii! Of course word of mouth has to be your number one form of advertising. If it's not, then you're doing something wrong.

Word of mouth is the reward the market gives you for doing a great job. It is social proof that you're doing well, because if you're offering a positive experience and results for your customers, then they should want to tell other people. If you're not making enough of an impression for them to bother telling anyone else, that's a problem. So yes, word of mouth should always be your number one form of advertising. But it can only reach so far so fast. It can only get as far as one person talking to one person at a time. So, if you want to grow at a faster rate and reach further than word of mouth can, or if you want to reinforce or change the story that is being told about you, that's where advertising comes in.

The danger of relying solely on word of mouth is that you are not controlling the story and people are more than twice as likely to share a bad experience they've had with a business than they are to share a good one. All of us have those times when we've been angry at a business, the service, the return policy, or something they handled poorly, or even something that a salesperson did or didn't do. And we've turned around and told people about it. But if you went in to shop for clothes and the clerk greeted you when you walked in, gave you just the right amount of assistance in finding things to try on, got you different sizes when you asked, and carried your chosen garments to the checkout, you likely wouldn't bother to tell people, "I had a pleasant experience at Banana Republic today."

That being the case, positive word of mouth is proof that you're doing something right, but it may not have the great reach you need to grow your business quickly enough.

THE WOW FACTOR:
GENERATING GREAT WORD OF MOUTH

In Chapter 2, we explored the fact that every business has a unique story, but not all of the attributes that make your store unique should be included in your advertising. Sometimes those benefits are better left for your paying customers to experience. When you surprise your customers and offer them an exceptional experience, that is when you will generate great word of mouth.

For example, you wouldn't talk about your level of customer service in your ads, but those little extras surprise and delight your customers when they visit you.

Although word of mouth shouldn't be the only way you advertise your business, it is the best place to start. Here are a few ways that you can generate positive word of mouth:

Offer a consistent service experience every time customers walk through the door. Give them just a little bit more than what they came in for (the hand massage while your hair color sets, the special flavored coffee—every time).

Engage customers in a unique, non-pushy way. Try having your staff greet customers without saying, "How can I help you?" Give them some time to shop around, pay attention to what they're looking at or talking about, and after a reasonable amount of time, strike up a conversation to answer questions they have about what they're looking at.

"Wow" your customers when they come in by doing something unexpected. As an example, the fishmongers at Pike Place Fish Market in Seattle are world-famous for their "wow." They have one guy taking the order, who yells it across the market to another guy who picks up the fish and flings it above the crowd where it's caught with ease and wrapped in newspaper before ceremoniously being presented to the customer. Between serving customers, they entertain themselves and the crowd of spectators by yelling and throwing fish back and forth to each other and getting customers to catch fish or give one a kiss.

Be mindful of what you want to create in the experience that will make them talk. At the radio station I worked for, we sometimes wowed our clients when they came in for meetings by decorating the boardroom in a theme that suited their business or personal hobbies and bringing in food and games to match the theme.

One time, when I was fairly new, I was getting ready to present a big sponsorship campaign to A&W Restaurants and I wanted to stand out from the many other more experienced media reps who were calling on them at the time. I went to one of their nearby locations and borrowed a serving tray and got some fry containers and burger wrappers and a fountain drink cup. I arrived at the presentation wearing orange and brown (the A&W colors), and presented the proposal to my clients on the tray, with the pages of the proposal hidden in the cup, burger wrapper, and fry box. They were impressed that I made the extra effort, and it contributed to their decision to commit to the sponsorship I was proposing.

Have more product knowledge than your customers are expecting. How many times have you asked an employee at a store about a product and they pulled out their mobile phone to Google it? You could've done that yourself, so it doesn't give off the best impression. Instead, have your staff trained and educated on your products so they can offer advanced knowledge and tips that you might not be able to find online.

Go out of your way to solve a problem when one arises for a customer. If you can make someone's day better by offering them a solution they might not have thought of, you will probably surprise that customer and inspire them to tell other people what happened.

A friend of mine was telling me about one of the numerous of times he broke his iPhone. He went into the Apple Store with a cracked screen and a grumpy mood. As he walked up to one of the employees, he said, "Can I get a new phone?" assuming he'd have to spend $1000 to replace it. The Apple employee asked, "Do you have AppleCare?" He told her he might have at one point, but that it was likely expired. And when she looked him up in their system, she said, "Yes it has, but we can extend it and replace your phone for $149." Then she asked, "When was the last time you backed up your phone?" "It's been a while." She proceeded to help him back up his phone to his computer, then kept it overnight, transferred the data from the old phone to a replacement phone at no charge, asked him to be there at 10:00 to pick up his new phone and had him out of there and on his way by 10:10.

My friend has told that story to dozens of people. Because of Apple's efforts to consistently "wow" their customers, they continue to prove they deserve the reputation they have. When your client or customer has a challenge, that's often the best opportunity to create a positive share-worthy experience.

We like to talk about fun and off-the-wall ways you can wow a client, but sometimes just being the constant, sure thing in our chaotic lives is enough. If you treat your customers well, deliver on your promises, handle objections properly, and consistently invite them to come back, that's better than trying to get attention with crazy stunts.

SOCIAL MEDIA

Social media is a fun, relatively new version of word-of-mouth on steroids. Your happiest customers can easily share their experience of your store, but not with only one person at a time; it can be more like 500–1000 people at a time.

As much as we'd like to think they do, though, people are not spending a lot of time on social media discussing their favorite stores and brands. In fact, they are online discussing everything *but* brands. In order to harness social media for your business, you have to take an active role in making those conversations happen. Here are some of the ways you can influence positive online word-of-mouth advertising and build a long-lasting relationship with your customers:

- Ask happy customers to post reviews or testimonials about their experience.

- Post work you've done for customers and (with their permission) tag them in the posts. They will be more likely to share it for their friends to see.

- Re-post customers' content.

- Thank customers if they re-post something of yours.

- Share charitable work your customers do.

- Send emails out to customers asking them to rate their experience with your business and then publish the data online.

Rather than just trying to sell your products on social media, start by putting your customers first and offering value. A good guideline when engaging on social media for your business is to follow the rule of thirds: a third of your posts should promote your business, a third should be for sharing content (stories and ideas from thought leaders in your industry or like-minded businesses), and a third should engage with your followers.

The best and scariest thing about social media is that it's a two-way conversation. It's awesome because you have instant access to your customers, but it's scary because it's just too easy for a disgruntled customer to share their bad review with a huge crowd of people online. Online reviews and social media posts to your friends are a very quick and easy way to vent your frustration. News of bad customer service experiences reach over twice as many people as praise.

Just last week, a friend of mine posted two pictures side by side of a reddish-brown, ugly bug on her Facebook feed. Her caption was: "Pic on left...file photo of a cockroach. Pic on right? Photo I took at [name of the restaurant] today. They are in the ladies room and the dining area. I have filed a complaint with public health and lo and behold... who got a negative rating on their last inspection for not being pest free?" As you can imagine, this negative online word-of-mouth will not be very good for the restaurant. A number of people commented and added to the story, and further down the list of comments my friend added, "Also mentioned it to the manager before I filed a complaint. Thought I would give them the benefit of the doubt, maybe they didn't know...his non-reaction spoke volumes." She gave the restaurant the opportunity to save themselves some of the fallout from this and they failed that too.

Here are some of the things you can do to minimize and properly handle negative comments and reviews online:

- First and foremost, get the word out about your company in the market the way you want the story to be told through your actions, networking, and advertising; the more positive the story is, the more it will outweigh the potential negative comment or two.

- Monitor your social media so you can respond to comments in a timely manner.

- When you receive a complaint online, don't get defensive. Acknowledge the complaint and indicate how you will make it right.

- Don't delete the comment unless it's offensive or inappropriate.

- Oh and don't have cockroaches in your restaurant!

Last fall, my husband and I took another trip to New York. We stayed at a hotel right in downtown Manhattan, a block from the Broadway shows we had come to see. It was a recently renovated, modern hotel, but there were a few surfaces in our room that clearly hadn't been dusted in a long time and one slightly grimy spot on one of the counters. It wasn't enough to bother complaining about, but it was enough to notice.

After we checked out and returned home, we got an email from the hotel asking us to fill out a short survey about our experience. In the survey, I noted that the cleanliness wasn't the best. Within a day, the general manager of the hotel emailed me apologizing. He thanked me for the feedback and said he'd let housekeeping know. He also took the liberty of refunding us $150 from our bill. Talk about a "wow"! We weren't asking for anything or expecting anything in return, but you can be sure we'll stay there next time we go and we'll tell people about it. How you handle a complaint can convert somebody into part of your tribe. I have a better feeling about that hotel now than I would have if things had gone right in the first place!

LAYER 1: THE FOUNDATION

Your advertising plan has to start somewhere. Once you establish how you will draw attention at your location, and you create a customer experience that is worthy of positive word of mouth, your next step is to develop the foundation of your advertising.

Remember, the goal of your advertising is to get yourself into the long-term memory of your potential clients; to become the brand that your customers think of first and feel the best about. You want to be top-of-mind so that when your customers need you, they know where to go.

Your foundation should be the media you use most often and most consistently, that allows you to achieve those three fundamental elements of advertising: CCF (consistency, creativity, and frequency) sight and sound, and online presence.

So, which media can achieve that? For Layer 1, we will look at TV and radio—intrusive media that broadcast your advertising—as well as search engine optimization (SEO), which is a passive medium that ensures you are easily found online when people are in the market for products in your category.

RADIO

There's a funny story being told about local radio these days. People are saying that nobody is listening anymore; that everyone has moved to satellite radio or online streaming channels, or that they all just listen to music on iTunes.

What's funny is that it's not true at all. Here are the facts (based on US data):

- Radio is the leading reach platform.[5]

- Ninety-three percent of us listen to AM/FM radio, which is higher than TV viewership (85%),[6] online streaming channels (47%),[7] and satellite radio listening (9%).[8]

- 265 million Americans age six and over listen to the radio at least once a week—66 million of whom are millennials.[9]

- The average listener tunes in for 12–17 hours each week.[10]

- Facebook reports to have 191 million users in the United States,[11] while 265 million Americans[12] tune in to local radio each week.

Do you remember the song "Video Killed the Radio Star" by The Buggles? If you were an 80s child or older, you would. First, it was supposed to be that video would kill the radio star, then the iPod was going to do it, and most recently, satellite radio and online streaming stations. But none of these have dampened the power of local radio because people listen to their community stations for the local connection. If you just want music, there's always been a choice for that: records, cassette tapes, CDs, iPods…but the reason people keep coming back to local radio is for what happens between the music. Then they choose the station based on the music they like best.

STRENGTHS

Radio is the most cost-effective and powerful way to achieve CCF for your business.

- **Consistency**—people are loyal to their favorite stations. They listen for hours each day and feel like they know the radio station's personalities. Since radio programs have such a loyal following, you can reach them with consistency year-round. You can speak to the same audience week in and week out, 52 weeks a year.

- **Creativity**—words are worth a thousand pictures. Without the constraints of the visual, you can craft your words to paint any picture you can imagine. And the best part about it is that when you do, the audience pictures themselves in that scene, customized to their world. "Theatre of the mind" has endless potential. To get somebody to act, you need to get them to picture themselves doing what you want them to do first, and the best way to do that is through sound.

- **Frequency**—the audience spends hours each week listening, often for eight hours a day, five days a week at work, so they will hear you with frequency. With the right schedule, you can reach the same listener at least three times per week and achieve that magic frequency we talked about. Radio is a "frequency medium," so for the price of one newspaper ad, you get multiple radio ads.

On top of the CCF benefits, radio stations generally don't charge you an extra fee for writing, production, or updates, so creating a commercial is essentially free. On top of that, writers and producers housed in radio stations can create commercials that are just as good (and often even better) than the national agencies, so your business benefits from the quality. Low cost of production coupled with unlimited creative potential allows you to present commercials that can tell your story the way you want to tell it.

Unlike with print ads where you could be surrounded by competitors' ads, with radio your ad stands alone. You can expect that your ad would not run next to a competitor's, so you have the audience's attention all to yourself. Radio broadcasters are adapting with the times and offer a range of online options that complement your radio advertising, such as ads that appear on their station's website and the ability for listeners to tune in online and on mobile apps.

The ability of radio to build brands through CCF so effectively and efficiently is one of the reasons I spent so many years working in radio advertising.

LIMITATIONS

Radio is great, but it's not for everyone. If your business doesn't have a big enough budget, you can get lost on a radio station. You need to find out from your local station how many ads a week you need to buy from them to achieve that frequency of three with the average listener. When your budget will allow you to buy enough for a viable schedule, 52 weeks a year, that's when you are big enough to buy radio to brand your business. If you can't buy all 52 weeks, start by trying to fill as much of the year as possible with short breaks and work your way up to year-round.

In major metropolitan cities, any traditional radio station may have too broad a geographic reach for your single-location store and might be cost-prohibitive for smaller advertisers. In some countries, streaming radio, like Spotify and Pandora, offers advertising space for purchase which can be demographically and geographically targeted. This may appear to be a good solution for you to reach your trading area through sound, however the minimum advertising investment is often quite large, listeners can pay to opt out of hearing commercials on some sites, and these stations are currently dominated by national brands.

The size of city you are in will greatly influence whether traditional radio is a viable option for you or if it is just too big.

How to use it

The average radio listener spends more than 12 hours per week with their favorite station. So, you can run a couple dozen commercials each week and have a good chance of reaching the same listener multiple times. If you can't afford that much frequency, there are ways to narrow your reach on a station by only purchasing ads in the morning show, on weekends, or in the evenings. Staying consistent with your message and the audience you have set out to reach will build your brand in the minds of listeners.

TELEVISION

Just like with radio, there is a funny story being told about TV these days. People are saying that nobody is watching anymore. And even if they are watching, they're skipping commercials using their DVR. But more likely than that, they are only watching Netflix and YouTube. Just like with radio, it's funny because it's not true.

Some say that we are in the golden age of TV. There are more shows, more channels, and more ways to watch than ever before. We can watch live or recorded, watch on our computer or our mobile device, or binge watch an entire series on Netflix over a weekend. All of this means that TV viewership is at an all-time high, just not in the same way as in the past.

Nielsen, the American company that measures audience size and composition for television, reports viewership in the tens of millions for broadcasts like NBC Sunday Night Football (22 million) and primetime shows like America's Got Talent (14.5 Million).[13] On top of that, they report:

- 296.8 million Americans have TVs in their homes and have traditional TV access.[14]

- Eighty-five percent of the population watches live TV at least once every week.[15]

- Viewership ranges from 14 hours per week (teens) to 29 hours per week (Gen Xers) to 40 hours per week (older adults). Overall the average American spends over five hours *each day* watching TV. Although these numbers have decreased over the past five years, this is still a significant amount of time spent with this medium.[16]

- Though viewership of streaming video online is on the rise, it appears to be complementing rather than replacing traditional TV, and traditional TV is still dominant in time spent viewing.

- Only about 11% of TV viewership is done via DVR as compared to watching live, which means even if all DVR viewers skipped the commercial, only 11% of viewers would be missed by advertisers.[17]

It's no secret that regular TV viewership is declining. There are simply so many other viewing options emerging that take viewers away. But even with Netflix and YouTube, TV still reaches 85% of households every week. Regardless of the slight decline, TV delivers a huge audience to advertisers and remains one of the most effective advertising media.

STRENGTHS

TV ads are powerful because they combine sight, sound, and motion. They make impressions similar to radio, but connecting with even more senses—all before you're in the market for the product or service. And since it is so versatile, you can achieve CCF with TV as well:

- **Consistency**—you can target a demographic within a TV audience and reach them 52 weeks per year.

- **Creativity**—you have 15–60 seconds in which to tell your story, set a scene, or get across an emotion.

- **Frequency**—TV, like radio, is a frequency medium in that it is designed to run multiple ads for each advertiser each week.

With a television ad, yours is the only one being played on that channel at that time and your ad would not run next to a competitor's, so you have the audience's eyes and ears all to yourself.

Television broadcasters are adapting with the times and offer a range of integrated online options that complement your TV advertising, such as ads that appear on their TV channel websites and at the beginning of their online streaming lineup. All of this contributes to extra impressions on your chosen audience.

LIMITATIONS

Though TV ads have a great impact because of the sight and sound aspect, as a local advertiser it can be difficult and expensive to buy a consistent schedule that will reach anyone with enough frequency. You also need to check the inventory that is available to a local advertiser, as often the national brands buy up the prime spots and local buyers are left with fringe times. TV has become a national advertiser-dominant medium.

If your business doesn't have a large enough budget to produce a high-quality commercial and purchase an adequate schedule, then TV is too big for you. Local ads tend to look like local ads, and so they don't measure up to the million-dollar production of the national brands. If your commercial runs right after a Macy's or Coca-Cola ad, the difference is noticeable—and not in your favor. Having said that, everyone has better access to improved technology all the time, so local ads are getting better and better.

HOW TO USE IT

The difference between a TV viewing audience and a radio listening audience is that you don't spend all of your time watching a certain TV channel. You don't say, "I'm an NBC fan, so I'm going to watch NBC for the day," where that is something you would say about your radio station. This means you'll want to buy TV ads differently than radio.

Buying a full-day rotation (meaning your ads would run scattered throughout the day) is not going to build any frequency with the same viewer. Instead, your TV rep can schedule your commercials so they run within programs that have a consistent demographic of viewers, so you have a better chance of reaching the same person with enough frequency each week. A sponsorship during the evening news or primetime spots in shows that appeal to females age 35–54 is an example of how you can build consistency and frequency with a specific segment of that TV station's audience, because the same person within that group is likely to watch more than one show targeted at her each week.

In addition, you can buy display ads on the TV station's web sites to create more impressions with your chosen audience, and those can be geographically targeted.

SEARCH ENGINE OPTIMIZATION (SEO)

Search engine optimization (SEO) is a strategy used to ensure that you show up as close to the top of the "free" or "organic" search listings as possible when someone searches for your business or category online. Typically, SEO refers to the search results for specific keywords on search engines like Google, Bing, or Yahoo.

Optimizing your search results involves strategies, tactics, and techniques to make sure your website is findable and credible to search engines and that it keeps up with the constantly changing criteria. Many web marketers focus nearly all their energy on optimizing search results for their clients. They want to make sure that if someone searches "Flooring Toronto," your flooring store will appear in the top 10 results.

STRENGTHS

The better your search rankings, the more likely you will be found online by people who aren't necessarily looking specifically for *your* business, but are looking for businesses in your category. You have a chance of being shopped when a customer searches your general category without a specific company in mind, meaning you will have a leg up on your competitors. Since most people do research online before making purchase decisions, the better your search rankings, the more likely you will be found by new customers and the greater your chances will be of getting their business.

LIMITATIONS

If you are a business with very little or no competition in your category in your trading area, you really don't need to worry about your ranking in Google and other search engines. If someone searched your business category and city name and you were one of only three that would appear, it doesn't matter if you are first, second, or third. For example, say you make custom railings and only two other companies in your trading area make custom railings. When "railings [your town]" is searched, all three of you will appear on the first page and most shoppers would check out all three of you. Is there a need to pay to be first instead of third?

If you do need to use SEO, the criteria that determines your search ranking is constantly changing and very difficult to keep up with. This means you have to keep current on what Google and other search engines are looking for or you will get left behind.

SEO makes sure you are *found* when someone searches your business category and doesn't have a specific business in mind. Though this is important, it is also very passive. It's much more beneficial to use active advertising that *reaches out* to people than it is to wait to be found.

If there are many businesses in your category in your city, you are listed among all of your competitors in search results with very little opportunity to stand out on the list unless the viewer has prior knowledge of your business from outside brand advertising. For example, if you're a mortgage broker and typing in "mortgage broker [your city]" results in three pages of listings, do you want to focus all your energy on getting to the top of the organic search results by keeping up with and adapting to the ever-changing rules of Google? Or would you rather brand your name in the community using media and online advertising, so instead of searching "mortgage broker [your city]" they search "Kelsey Woods Realtor [your city]." Guess what? You're the only one that shows up! For the people who are searching your name online, your outside branding has done its job. Those who are searching your category have not been effectively reached with your advertising message.

When you invite people to *seek you out*, rather than waiting to be *found*, you're much better off in the long run. On top of that, if you have brand recognition in the market, even if someone searches "mortgage broker [your city]," you have a better chance of being *picked* out of the list if they recognize your name. Why do you think people running for small city council or school board positions run billboards? They do it in hopes that when you see their name on the ballot among a bunch of other people you've never heard of, you'll pick them because they're familiar.

HOW TO USE IT

If you decide SEO would be beneficial to your business, there are countless ways to improve your ranking. Unless you are an SEO expert or well-versed in web marketing, you would be best served by having an expert implement your SEO. However, if you only want to do the bare minimum, here are a few things you can do that take little technical know-how:

- Publish content that is relevant to the categories you want to be found under (blogs, YouTube videos, etc.)
- Update your content regularly
- Have your site linked to other relevant sites
- Make sure your website is mobile-friendly (when your website is viewed from a mobile phone, it is formatted to be read and navigated easily on the small screen)

You can also spend some money to have your business show up at the top of the list in the paid search section. You bid on the keywords you'd like to own (for example, if you were a caterer you could bid on "caterer," "delivery," "lunch," "chef"). Then, when someone searches those keywords, you appear at the top or right side in the sponsored links zone with a little green icon that says "ad" next to your listing. And then you pay each time someone clicks your link. This is not an SEO technique, but it is a way to appear at the top of a search results page. This can be effective in some circumstances, but studies show that most people skip past these listings and go right to the "organic" results.

LAYER 2: FREQUENCY

Layer 2 advertising is focused on telling a short story with high frequency.

Once you have your foundation established and your name is starting to become recognizable in your space, you can start implementing elements and media that fall into the frequency layer. This layer is particularly useful if people do not need to hear a lot of your story to get your message across (like "We're a greenhouse and open for the season!") or if you are telling your detailed story elsewhere and you simply want to remind people about you.

Layer 2 features outdoor advertising (like billboards and bus shelters) and paid online advertising (like banner ads and paid search).

OUTDOOR (OUT-OF-HOME) ADVERTISING

Outdoor advertising means anything that is on display, well, outdoors. This includes billboards, ads on buses, posters in bus shelters and on bus benches, as well as those inside your subway car, wrapped around a taxi, and all the bright flashing color in Times Square. Sandwich boards and neon signs in front of your business, your painted store window, and your company vehicles wrapped with your logo also count. Like other traditional advertising, outdoor advertising is still an effective way of reaching an audience:[18]

- Out-of-home media reaches people regardless of how they consume other media and is ever-present.

- Over half of American adults have noticed a roadside billboard in the past month.

- Sixty-five percent of adults noticed a billboard directing them to a nearby store, business, or restaurant.

- Fifty-five percent of consumers who noticed directional billboards changed their plans to visit the business advertised.

- Nearly a quarter of those who saw a billboard in the last month made a purchase at the business advertised.

STRENGTHS

The biggest benefit of outdoor advertising is the frequency you can achieve. The two main ways to achieve frequency with outdoor advertising are:

1. **Static ads.** With a standard billboard, the same person could drive or walk past it multiple times a week and you can buy multiple locations.

2. **Moving ads.** You can buy transit ads (sides of buses, etc.) with a high frequency and put ads on multiple buses for a reasonable price, so you will have many ads rolling around your community.

Static ads, like billboards, bus shelters, and your storefront are great because you can pinpoint a specific area of town where you want your message to be seen. If your business is relevant to your downtown core, or a specific suburb of your city, you can target this market by placing static ads in that location. In a major city, when TV or radio may reach too broad of an audience, you can target your specific neighborhood with billboards and bus shelter ads.

On the other end of the spectrum, transit ads have a wider reach because they travel across the city into several neighborhoods. This means you are more likely to reach many more people, so they are beneficial when you want as many people as possible to see you, or when your customer base is not limited to a single geographical location.

LIMITATIONS

The creative message you can send is limited with outdoor advertising. People are speeding by the ad and so you need to be able to get the message across in five words or less—that's how many they will likely see or have time to read. If you can get enough of your story across with an impactful image, a few words, and your logo, this can work great. However, if you have more explaining to do, it can be much too limiting.

I remember stopping my car under a billboard in a parking lot and I could barely read the text from right underneath it. Because I work in advertising, I tend to care more about what ads say and I try to figure this stuff out, so I made an effort to read it. It looked like they took an event poster and blew it up for a billboard. The advertiser tried to get too much information across on a media that is not designed for that. Most people aren't like me, so the fact that it was hard to read means most people would immediately dismiss it. Nobody cares enough to slow down and try and figure out the message.

If you already have Layer 1 taken care of, you could include a key phrase from your audio messaging as a reminder. If you choose to go this route, keep in mind that:

- The message can't be changed very often without spending money on new production.

- Depending on the city and area, there can be a lot of outdoor ad clutter, making it difficult to be noticed in the sea of other ads. Be selective of your location to make sure it's not overrun.

- If a static billboard has the same ad on it for too long, it starts to get ignored, so you'll have to move your billboard ad around at regular intervals to different locations or use ads on public transit that move around for you.

- Digital billboards—the flashy, blindingly white digital screens that have popped up over the past few years—are noticeable because of their brightness, but usually you are rotated among 10 or more ads, reducing the frequency of impressions to one tenth of what a static billboard would give you. What you lose in frequency you will have to make up in consistency, so leave your digital billboard in the same location for longer. On the other hand, those digital billboards in Times Square? I think they reach a few people...

How to use it

Using static and moving ads can be an easy way to get a short version of your message in front of more faces. Here are a few tips to make your outdoor campaign as successful as possible:

- Use stationary outdoor ads in high traffic areas. This could mean targeting the neighborhoods surrounding your business location or buying ads all the way down one main street.

- Make sure they face the flow of traffic, and that they're not covered by trees! (This actually happens if you aren't careful).

- Move your billboard location regularly because it will stop being noticed if it stays in one spot.

- Buy transit ads (buses, subways, etc.) with high frequency by buying as many as your budget will allow at a time. You can own the interiors of entire buses or subway cars to really make a splash, or wrap the entire outside of a bus like a huge traveling billboard for your business.

- Outdoor is best used for a very simple message, a one-sentence call to action, or to act as a reminder and reinforcement of the other more detailed advertising you are doing.

Paid online advertising

Paid online advertising includes banner and display ads that appear at the top and side of web pages, paid search ads that you see at the top of search results pages, and ads that appear on social media platforms like Facebook, Twitter, and Instagram.

Here are some of the main players:

- **Promoted or boosted posts on social media**—posts you've created yourself, that you pay to show to your followers.

- **Banner and display ads on websites**—the rectangular ads that appear on the top, side, or bottom of various websites. The space is shared among a few dozen advertisers and each advertiser's ad appears in rotation.

- **Paid social media ads**—the ads that advertise companies and products in your newsfeed on Facebook, Twitter, and other platforms. They can also appear on the right sidebar on Facebook if you're viewing it on your PC.

- **Sponsored search listings**—listings and ads that appear at the top or on the side of the search results page on Google and other search engines.

- **Pre-roll on streaming video**—a video commercial that plays before streaming a TV show (on the network's website) or YouTube video. You'll recognize these as the ads that often give the option to "skip ad in 5 seconds…"

The Internet is absolutely massive with billions of actions being taken each and every day. Here are some interesting facts:

- Eighty-eight percent of the population uses the Internet (that's 290 million users in the US).[19]

- People spend almost 5 hours per day on the Internet on their PCs, and almost 2 hours per day online using mobile devices.[20]

- A third of the time spent online is on social media. The average person will spend almost 2 hours per day on social media, with the most time on YouTube followed by Facebook.[21]

- Seventy-eight percent of Americans have a social network profile.[22]

STRENGTHS

Paid online advertising can achieve frequency with your messaging. Similar to outdoor ads, you can offer a very short message with an interesting image or reinforce a message that you are sending out with other media like television.

SOCIAL MEDIA

You can make impressions on your audience daily on social media, and you can be creative with articles, video, images, and conversation. It is highly targetable, as you can choose your audience based on everything from their marital status to their occupation to their interest in yoga. Social media opens the door for two-way communication, building a deeper relationship with your audience and offering the opportunity for your viewers to interact with you by liking or commenting. Social media marketing can be very cost effective and you can update or change your message in real time.

DISPLAY AND BANNER ADS

You can make impressions on people with a great deal of frequency by strategically placing display ads on websites and specifically targeting your audience. You decide which websites your ads will appear on and which search terms will result in your ad being displayed, and you can get your ads in front of people who have recently shown interest in your business category online.

Social media and display ad services both allow you to get more visitors to your website, bringing them a step closer to doing business with you. You can control your spending by setting a specific budget to pay per click or per impression, then you only pay when people see your ads and your ads no longer display when you've reached your budget limit.

LIMITATIONS

SOCIAL MEDIA

One of the most important and most overlooked considerations with regards to social media is that some business categories are suited to be on social media and others are not. If you are a clothing store, a trendy restaurant, or you offer women's empowerment workshops, people would likely welcome your posts or display ads into their social feed because they are social in nature; they are all lifestyle-enhancing and people see value in being updated on new apparel you have in stock or events that they want to attend. But if you are a transmission shop, or a mining company, most people don't have much desire to socialize with you online and your post seems more like an interruption. Before you post, think about whether you are adding value to your audience's online social time.

Even a transmission shop or mining company could offer some good content once in a while (transmission maintenance tips, a report on the environmental impact of mining, etc.), but that would be difficult to maintain on a consistent basis and it is still not social in nature. So, when deciding if social media marketing is right for you, consider the way people will use your business and the way they use social media.

If you're a commodity or a need, people are less inclined to "socialize" with your brand online. For example, I don't ever want to have to go to a transmission repair shop and I don't want to be reminded about that service while I'm checking in with my friends online. If I do need to get my transmission fixed, I don't want to then be reminded about it again and again—it's not a happy memory for me. I use this as an example because I did need to replace the transmission on a vehicle a number of years ago. The shop had a neon sign in front inviting people to "like us on Facebook and Twitter!" Why. The. Hell…?

As a wise friend of mine says, advertising on social media can be like putting up a poster at a rock concert. It might look really nice, but that's not what people are there for. If you're not adding value or interest for the viewer, you're going to be ignored.

As a local business, targeting ads or boosting posts on social media casts a relatively small net. If boosted posts are all that your budget will allow, and your business is suited to it, then they are a good place to start. But if you have the budget to go beyond targeted local Facebook audiences, by all means, cast a bigger net and you will catch more fish.

Any mass media will reach a larger chunk of the market, giving more people the chance to do business with you. To be clear, if your target audience is on a national scale, online is the gateway to millions of potential customers. But if you are a local, brick and mortar business, the percentage of your city that you will make an impact with on social media is limited.

More often than not, business owners put *way* too much weight on the importance of their social media posts and ads and not enough time face to face with their customers and community or sending their message out to people beyond the computer screen. If you cannot imagine coming up with new content every day involving the single product you produce, but you know that if you are in front of customers in person more you sell more, it's likely that your time is better spent out there instead of behind your computer desk. Overall, consider how much time you should be spending on this and how much should be spent out on the sales floor selling your products to customers.

DISPLAY AND BANNER ADS

A limitation of display ads is the ad avoidance factor. Since the average Internet user has become accustomed to where display ads appear on a site, banner ads at the top, rectangular ads on the side of a website, and especially ad zones at the bottom of a web page are often easily avoided—the eye goes to the content and ignores ad zones, just like in newspaper.

If your ad zone is generally avoided and you are in rotation with 39 other ads in the same space, how is the same person going to have any chance of repeat impressions? On top of that, 26% (and always increasing) of web surfers use ad blockers on their PCs and 15% on their mobile devices so you won't reach them because this portion of the population doesn't even see ads at all.

HOW TO USE IT

SOCIAL MEDIA

On social media, there are two different forms of advertising: paid display ads and boosted posts.

When you generate content on social media platforms (Facebook posts, tweets, photos and videos on Instagram, etc.), you can "boost" your post by paying to show that content to a wider audience. This means that more people will see your content.

If you are already using social media to engage with your customers, it can be advantageous to boost posts to get more viewers and reach a wider audience. Social media is a "pay to play" platform now more than ever. When you create a free, or "organic" post on your business Facebook page, for example, between 2–6% of your followers will see that post on their news feed (so, if you had 1000 followers, only 20–60 of them will see your post and the rest would have to visit your page to see it).[23] Same goes for your organic post on Twitter. No social media option will allow more than 20% of your followers to see any of your free "organic" posts on their feed, and this is expected to go down to zero in the near future.

This is because there is far more content being created every minute by your friends and by companies than you could possibly read when you log in. Content has to be vetted before it hits your news feed. These platforms are meant to be *social*, so if the manager allowed all advertisers to reach you for free, then all you'd see would be business posts, and you wouldn't want to spend time on there anymore.

So, for a very small investment, you can pay to promote or boost your social media posts. This allows you to reach not only more of your followers, but their friends and their friends' friends. You can geo-target (target certain areas of town) and narrow down your audience by demographics and interests. You can reach your chosen groups a number of times each week, so if you have a limited budget, this allows you to focus your efforts on the people who most closely match your ideal customer. You can also set daily spend limits so you control your spending.

The other option on social media is to pay for display ads. Rather than boosting content you've already created, you will generate ad copy and pay to display it to whichever demographics and interests you choose. Just like with boosts, you can set a budget for the campaign and target your audience as much as you want.

DISPLAY AND BANNER ADS

Display and banner ads are typically created using ad services like Google's AdWords. You create ad copy and then pay to display your ads on websites that are relevant to your business. For most businesses, re-targeting ads is the best way to take advantage of display and banner ad opportunities.

You know when you visit a website to look up a product, and then that product or company seems to appear on every ad on every website you visit for the next week? That's the company re-targeting their ads to you. Basically, the ad service displays your ads to people who have recently visited your website or searched your category. It is the most effective way to apply an online display ad campaign because it creates frequency with people who have already shown interest in your product.

VIDEO

Half of the time people spend online on mobile devices is spent watching videos. Of all social media platforms, people spend the most time on YouTube at an average of 40 minutes each day. If you post videos and video ads, you have a better chance of being selected and having the viewer spend some time with you. Although we'll talk more about video in Chapter 6, keep in mind that video has the potential to add the *creative* elements of movement and sound to online advertising that is missing from static online ads.

EXECUTION

When it comes to online advertising of any kind, only start it if you can commit to consistently doing a good job of it. This means creating high-quality posts and ads yourself, designating a staff member who knows your business and will keep on top of it, or hiring a third-party to do it for you.

There is a tendency among business owners, especially older ones, to hire young kids who "know their stuff" to do social media for them, but this is usually detrimental because these kids often don't understand marketing, don't know your business well enough, and don't create high quality, professional content. It's better not to participate in online marketing than to do a poor job of it, so if you are hiring a social media manager, be sure to find someone who understands marketing and who is willing to work with you to learn about your business.

To figure out if putting all your efforts into Layer 2 will be right for you, consider how long your message is and how familiar your audience already is with your brand. Outdoor advertising and paid online advertising are both great ways to remind your audience what you've told them in your Layer 1 advertising, or to get across a simple message with a few words and an image. If either of these sound like you, you're in a great position for Layer 2 advertising.

LAYER 3: FOLLOW-UP COMMUNICATIONS

Once you have set the foundation and you've found elements that work to increase the frequency with which your audience is exposed to your message, your next job is to follow up with the customers you've gained. This layer implements systems you can use to build a deeper relationship with them and maintain top-of-mind awareness. We know that keeping an existing customer is easier than gaining a new one, so continuing to build that relationship with your customers is important to your advertising success.

Social media and newsletters are two excellent (and popular) ways to keep in touch with your existing customers. Both allow for you to update your people on what's new, remind them that you are still around when they need you, and invite them to keep coming back.

SOCIAL MEDIA

Small businesses can use social media as a way to follow-up with their customers by posting regularly on social pages and providing valuable content, then boosting it. Be careful not to just post sell messages, though. One of the massive benefits of social media platforms is that two-way communication channel. Social media allows you to reach out to your existing customers (since they already have "liked" or "followed" you) and build a lasting relationship that will keep them coming back.

STRENGTHS

As mentioned above, the main strength of social media for follow-up communication is that you get to build a relationship with your customer outside of the store. Now, rather than only communicating with them when they are making purchases or seeing your ads, you can engage with them online. You can create content that is relevant to them and to your products, share more about your business and the story you want to tell, and hear from them about what they like or what they would want to see improved.

When you build those relationships with your customers, you have a chance to include them in your tribe. You become part of their lifestyle, and they become your biggest advocates. That's why social media marketing is becoming such a big deal in the world of advertising—and deservedly so.

LIMITATIONS

As great as social media is for building relationships with your customer, it can also become a time suck, and that is the main drawback of engaging online. Although there are clear benefits, the owner of a business is likely to have much more valuable "work" to do than respond to comments and generate content.

While this issue can be overcome by hiring a social media manager, not everyone has the budget for that, and those who do may get better returns on their money by putting it into intrusive media that can deliver CCF.

The beauty of social media being two-way communication can also be the curse. If you are committed to having your business participate on social platforms, you also have to commit to managing negative feedback in a timely and constructive manner. Bad customer service experiences put people off, and when it's shared on social media, it's there for the world to see.

If you can manage your social time while also effectively responding to negative feedback, though, your business can benefit from connecting and following-up with your customers.

How to use it

If your products or services are conducive to interaction online, you may find that social media is a good way to spend your time and money to keep top-of-mind with your customers. Here are some ways small businesses have effectively engaged with their customers online:

- Clothing stores post featured pieces or new arrivals and frequently have customers come in the same day to purchase the item that was posted.

- In the winter, Eb's Source for Adventure posts the cross country ski conditions and the type of ski wax that should be used in those conditions. In the summer, they post articles featuring great camping, hiking, or paddling spots that are close to our city.

- A greenhouse might post gardening tips specific to their climate, weather, and season. As an amateur gardener, I can always learn more about how and when to prune my perennials, how to store my root vegetables in the winter, and "is this a weed or a plant?" This information is useful and associates that greenhouse with gardening expertise.

- A bakery or restaurant could post "today's specials" to their Facebook and Twitter accounts, keep their store top-of-mind and post photos of meals right before lunchtime.

- Most businesses can re-post customer content and reviews, which can get people talking about you and provide social proof that you are a great place to shop.

- Business owners can share content from thought-leaders, which can add value and provide useful information on how to use products, which products you might want to buy, and what the seasonal trends are in your category.

In terms of best practices with social posts, you will generally get more engagement with a post if you include a picture, and even more if you include a video. If your business lends itself to it, you can even post pictures of your customers involved in something going on at your store and tag them (with their permission of course).

TEXT MESSAGE MARKETING

It's worth noting that sending updates and sale information via text messages or SMS to customers has grown in popularity. Over 90% of text messages are read within one minute. Likely only your biggest fans will sign up for text messages from your company or keep subscribed for any length of time, but you can be fairly certain they'll read the messages you send.[24]

NEWSLETTERS

Newsletters are the paper or email feature pieces you send out to your customers on a monthly or quarterly basis. These, like your free social media posts, are a way to stay in touch with your customers; they're not a way to reach a new audience.

Campaign Monitor reports that email marketing is the number-one choice of marketers worldwide. In 2016, open rates of email marketing reached 68%, and yet many retailers don't collect email addresses from customers. It is valuable to set up a system for collecting email addresses from your customers so you can continue to communicate directly with them.[25]

STRENGTHS

Of all the ways to keep in contact with their tribe, business owners tell me that their newsletters prove to be the most effective. Paper newsletters sent in the mail cut through the clutter because they are personally addressed and are rare these days. Email newsletters are seen and well-read because most people check their email every day, multiple times a day.

The biggest strength of newsletters is their creative content opportunities—a newsletter is a great place to tell your story or position your company as the experts or go-to guys in your field. Because it's not an ad, people will take more time reading it.

A paper newsletter is relatively inexpensive to print and mail, and an email newsletter is very cost-effective as well. MailChimp seems to be the e-newsletter provider of choice right now because it is very easy to use, plus it's free for up to 2000 email subscribers.

LIMITATIONS

The greatest limitation of a newsletter is the time it takes to put everything together. If you are into this sort of thing, you can easily get caught up adding as much value as possible and may enjoy creating the perfect newsletter each month. However, if it's not your thing at all, the task can seem daunting.

If you find you don't have the time or desire to put together your newsletter yourself, there are services that will sell content for you to use for your business category. You could also hire a "ghost writer" for your newsletter pieces and look like a genius while offering valuable information to your interested customers! These services, of course, will increase your costs.

HOW TO USE THEM

Your newsletter is an opportunity to add even more value for your customers. You should use it to offer tips, articles, and other material that your reader will find useful. You can also announce changes and updates to your store or your product lines.

A newsletter is an effective way to position yourself as the expert in your category. If you're a home service provider, you could offer things like a list of questions to ask a plumber before you hire them, or a checklist of things to do each year to make sure your home heating and cooling system is in good repair and ready each season. You could even run a monthly contest for your customers and announce the winners in the next issue.

To start a newsletter, you'll have to have a mailing list. Have your staff ask each customer at the till if they are on, or would like to join, your newsletter mailing list and you'll increase your list size (and your reach) with every issue. You can also invite your social media followers and web visitors to sign up for the newsletter.[26]

LAYER 4: EXTRA BLASTS

Layer 4 rests on top of all the other layers and periodically provides an extra blast to your advertising that enhances what you're *already* doing. A one-off or quarterly impression using these vehicles is not going to build enough top-of-mind awareness to replace any of the other layers, but it can supplement your base branding in the market.

Extra blasts can have two basic purposes: to build on your base layers of advertising (Layers 1, 2, and 3), or to help you maintain a light presence in the market when you already have plenty of business. If you're the former, and you've already set up what you need in Layers 1, 2, and 3, you might start feeling like you want or need a supplement to your base branding throughout the year. If you're the latter, you might find that all the other layers are a bit too aggressive. This is where magazines, newspapers, and direct mailers come in.

MAGAZINES

Magazines are an excellent way to add a little boost to the work you're already doing because they go out monthly, quarterly, or annually and allow you to reach a specific audience, depending on the topic and reach of the particular publication.

When we're talking about magazine advertising as an option for a local business, we're not talking about the big national magazines like *Time* or *People*. Instead, we're looking at your local or regional lifestyle magazines and home or special interest publications. When you choose well, you can reach a targeted group of people with similar interests, or ones in your immediate location. Since you're not a national brand, you don't need the reach of those big magazines, so sticking with smaller options helps you efficiently reach your local audience.

STRENGTHS

Advertising in magazines can offer a nice compliment to your regular advertising. Print advertising in publications represents your brand in a unique, professional-looking way. Here are some of the benefits to magazine advertising:

- You can reach a large audience with magazines. They sit on people's coffee tables and it is said that at least three different people will read the same magazine, and even more if it's sitting in a doctor's office waiting room, for example.

- You can display some of your work to show the quality of your products. For example, a kitchen renovation company can show photos of their most impressive project to give the viewer an idea of the scope of their work.

- Print delivers the visual representation of your brand—the logo, colors, images, wording, and font you choose for your ad, and even the style of the publication can help shape the image you're trying to portray.

- You can target special interest groups with magazines. If it is a specialty magazine, like one focused on home design, people who are getting ready to build a house or renovate may keep the magazine for reference throughout their project.

- A premium, glossy magazine can show off your brand in high quality.

LIMITATIONS

The main drawback of magazine advertising is that you cannot reach a magazine audience with frequency. Even if it's a monthly magazine, that's only twelve impressions in the year. And more often, local magazines are published quarterly or even less often. For the same reason, it's hard to build consistency with the audience. Even if you are advertising in every issue, will the same person read each one and notice your ad every time?

Recall is highest for print ads when the reader is in the market *today* for your product or service, but is more often overlooked by the rest of the readers who you've paid to reach. Unlike radio and TV, you don't have the benefit of sound to get your message ingrained in people's memories.

Magazines can be a fun and fancy way to promote your business, but if you need to build awareness and your budget does not reach far enough to cover at least one of the base layers, focus on those first before going this direction. Magazine advertising has its benefits, but it is more of a nice to have than a need.

Some magazines offer advertorials, which are articles that are purchased by the advertiser. They allow you to include a lot of information about your company and your brand, but most reputable magazines won't run those types of stories, or if they do, they'll only run a couple and clearly indicate that they are paid advertisements. If you are tempted to buy one of these features, consider putting all of that information on your website instead, and place an eye-catching ad in the magazine that invites readers to visit your site for more information. Magazines that are almost 100% ads are not very well-read and this is often what happens when magazines accept advertorials.

HOW TO USE THEM

Advertising in magazines is much like any other advertising. Start by selecting a magazine that has the right feel for your business. Make sure it reaches the audience you need it to reach and that it is distributed in your local area. Try to get information from the publisher about the circulation of the magazine—are they mailed out? Where to? Are they sitting at coffee shops or in stacks on newsstands for people to pick up? Are they only read by students? Does the audience they reach fit within your wheelhouse?

Once you choose a magazine, try to have your ad placed close to a relevant article that relates to your company, if possible, and have it tie into the style of the article. If you can manage that, you will be able to reach the most interested readers and form connections between the article and your business. If you can't get real estate right next to a relevant article, find out where your ad will be placed. If it's a business card-sized ad that will be lumped in the back with dozens of other business card-sized ads...well...why do people do that?

Look at a magazine ad as a way to punctuate your messaging to the market on a periodic basis. Do not expect it to break down your doors with an ongoing influx of customers. That's not its job. However, there are a few cases in which magazine advertising can be your main method of reaching your audience:

- **When you are already too busy to handle a significant increase in customer traffic.** A hair salon I worked with was booked up 10–12 weeks in advance. They didn't need Layer 1 advertising 52 weeks a year. That would simply be inviting more people in just to be turned away at the door—not necessarily good for business! So, they skipped the first three layers of advertising and focused on Layer 4; they did large ads in lifestyle magazines and the odd promotion or charitable sponsorship on the radio. Those kept his name in the market, but on a less aggressive basis than a high-frequency campaign.

- **When you are a specialty niche store.** If you are, for example, a quilting supply store, it makes complete sense for you to advertise primarily in a quilting magazine and it would not likely make sense to be on a mass-appeal media like TV. If you know that most people in your audience subscribe to a trade magazine, presence in that magazine is a good thing—maybe even *the best* thing—for your business.

Magazines can deliver information and showcase your brand in a visual way. They can also add an extra highlight to your ongoing advertising in other media and position you in the business category or niche market you'd like to be aligned with. Some of these same objectives can be achieved when you advertise in newspaper publications.

NEWSPAPERS

The truth is that daily newspapers are a dying breed. Local papers have been shutting down from coast to coast because of declining subscriptions and ad revenue. Readership of daily papers has been cut in half over the past 10 years. The most recent dailies to close are the *Daily News* in Nanaimo, BC, the *Guelph Mercury* in Guelph, ON, and the *Pittsburg Tribune-Review*.[27] These are just the newest of hundreds of closures over the last decade. Canada's biggest newspaper chain, Postmedia, reported losses of $352.5 million last year.[28] National papers like *National Post*, *The New York Times*, and *The Wall Street Journal* are scrambling to restructure, gain traction with online revenue, and keep afloat.[29]

People of our generation don't read the daily paper over breakfast like they did back in the day. If you don't think that's true, just get up early tomorrow morning and watch for your paper boy. How many homes does he stop at to deliver the paper? Every second one? Every fifth? Our lifestyles have changed. We are all busier and in more of a hurry. On top of that, we get our news as it happens on the Internet and on the radio, so we don't have to wait for the morning paper to tell us about what happened yesterday. Though your community may still have a daily paper, there's a good chance that their sales reps don't even bring up advertising in the printed version, as they are focused on trying to grow their online platform.

However, there is still a conversation to be had about local advertisers in newspapers (and not just as a delivery vehicle for flyers!). Though bigger city papers are shrinking in readership, they still do have readers (in fact in 2016, 66 million Americans were still reading the print version of their daily paper).[30] Many readers appreciate the quality of reporting offered by newspaper journalists that just cannot be matched through online news sources. Over half of seniors and older adults still read the paper, which is important for advertisers who want to reach the older market. Small town papers are still very well-read in their communities. Like magazines, many industry publications (like *The Western Producer*, focusing on agriculture in western Canada) have a large readership.

Another reason newspaper is a relevant conversation is that we're not talking about just the traditional daily papers. There are neighborhood papers, weekly papers, commuter papers (handed to you as you board the subway), and lifestyle papers. These all play a different role in our markets and can't all be painted with the same brush.

Commuter papers are good if you do business in a commuter city, because people will pick up the paper as they hop onto the subway. It will usually have their attention for 30 minutes or so as they head to work. An opportunity to advertise in a paper like this will get many eyes on your message and can actually give you some good exposure. This is great if you have a busy transit system (especially subways), but not very effective in cities where most people drive to work.

Lifestyle papers are those weekly or monthly papers that target university students or hipsters or the "buy local" crowd. They do some fun and interesting things to get their readers involved in their business by running contests for the "best-of" in each business category, like tapas restaurants, mortgage brokerages, and coffee shops in the city. That builds a lot of buzz as the nominees rally their friends to vote for them. Some of the neighborhood papers feature businesses in their area in stories over and above the advertising a business can purchase.

STRENGTHS

Despite a decrease in overall readership in the past decade, advertising in newspapers does have some benefits. Just like with magazines, newspapers won't likely be your main advertising focus, but they can be a supplement to give you a little boost once in a while. Newspaper advertising offers:

- **Space to include more information.** While most other advertising is better at persuasion, newspaper is best for education or relaying information. So, if you would like to include a huge list of the products you carry and their prices in a full-page ad, then you can do that (if you have the budget).

- **Placement in a relevant section.** You can buy ad space in a section that is specifically related to your business category. For example, some realtors still see good results from listing properties in the real estate section of the paper once a week.

- **Physical, portable ads.** It's still gratifying when people come into your store holding your ad for a product they would like to purchase. It makes you feel like people are seeing and responding to it.

- **Coupons.** You can place coupons in your ad to drive some short-term traffic to your store. Unlike most other advertising, people can cut your ad out of the paper and bring it in with them.

LIMITATIONS

Although the biggest drawback is pretty clear—that daily newspaper readership is shrinking—there are a few others that you will want to take into consideration before putting money into newspaper ads. They are:

- Just like with magazines, people are more likely to notice a newspaper ad if they are in the market for your product right now. They will not likely remember seeing the ad when they think about buying a product in six months.

- Daily newspaper ads are expensive when you consider that each ad is only one single impression and that readership is down. If you look at cost per impression, it's much more expensive to reach one newspaper reader than to reach one broadcast media listener or viewer.

- With a newspaper ad, you could be placed on the same page as all your competitors. What will be in your ad that will make them choose you over anyone else? Is your ad bigger? Do you have a better offer? It is hard to compete based on a print ad alone.

- Building consistency using newspaper advertising is expensive and it's not a frequency medium. At most, you have a frequency of one each day, if the same person reads the paper every day. If it's only periodically produced, obviously the frequency goes down.

- Creativity is limited. You can get across facts and information, but it's much harder to elicit emotion with a print ad. Without audio (voice and music that makes you feel a certain way), you don't hit on emotion. Since we make purchases based on our emotions then justify them with logic, newspaper advertising is much less impactful than a medium that includes sound.

- It's an information delivery vehicle, not a branding tool.

If you want to be in a newspaper, consider it an *extra* impression or an opportunity to tell readers about a specific product or service. If you are expecting to become a household name by running a business card-sized ad in a paper each week, you will be disappointed.

How to use them

Although our main focus here is on branding and not sale event advertising, a good use for a daily newspaper would be to advertise a sale when you want to list multiple items and their discounted prices. You can't do that as easily on radio or with a billboard.

If you have a new product to feature each week, you can do that in the paper fairly easily. As long as you have the budget to advertise on a regular basis, this can be a good way to build interest in your product line.

Just like in magazines, if you are in a niche market, your presence in a publication in that niche would target a select audience. Ads in an agricultural newspaper, for example, would be great if your business targets farmers.

Many of the best uses of newspaper ads, however, can be achieved on your website and on social media. As always, be sure to assess the benefits and drawbacks as they relate to your specific advertising goals to determine your best course of action.

DIRECT MAIL

In 2016 in the US, businesses spent about $9.5 billion on direct mail advertising. Although it might seem like an overly saturated medium, it remains popular with small businesses, especially those that are relatively new.

According to the 2015 BrandSpark Canadian Shopper study, 74% of grocery shoppers said they prefer print flyers that they can quickly flip through, while only 26% said they preferred reading digital flyers online.[31]

Direct mail includes newspaper flyers, leaflets, and door-hangers that are dropped at every house in a neighborhood.

STRENGTHS

If you are a new business, direct mail can be a great way to introduce yourself to the neighborhood. Because the message can be as long or short as you want, you can use flyers to announce sales, list products you sell, tell readers about your business, show off projects or products you are particularly proud of, or offer coupons readers can bring into the store. They are targetable to whichever neighborhoods you choose—your local area or new markets.

Not only are the ads themselves versatile in both length and quality, but these ads are delivered right to your customers' doors. This means they don't even have to go anywhere or pick up another publication to hear about you and see what you offer.

LIMITATIONS

While there are a few notable benefits, like any advertising medium, they aren't effective in all situations. Some limitations include:

- They share the same creative limitations as all other print media in that they are good for information delivery, but not for persuasion and emotion.

- They are usually mixed in with a pile of junk mail and people often toss them into the recycling bin without ever looking at them or noticing what's there.

- You cannot build consistency in an economical way with flyers; reaching the masses with flyers would be very cost prohibitive.

- And those coupon packs that are in shrink-wrapped plastic? I can't understand how they're still a thing! Does anyone use them?

- Lastly and most importantly, your flyer reaches your customers with a frequency of one. If they are not in the market right now for what you sell, they are not going to keep that flyer and think of you six months down the road when they do need you. This medium is good to punctuate a branding campaign or serve as a one-time announcement, but it is not a household name builder.

How to use it

Flyers can be an economical way to blanket your area when you are new or introduce an upcoming promotion or event. Sending out three or four deliveries in a row to let people know you're now doing business in their neighborhood or that something big is happening is a targeted and relatively inexpensive strategy.

Flyers can also be a way for take-out restaurants to get their entire menu into the hands of potential customers with the hope that people will keep your menu around their house and refer to it when they need to order something.

Some companies have spent a bit more money to send 3D mailers in an effort to stand out from their competitors. This is usually in the form of a sample of their product or a novelty item with a message attached, like sending a packet of flower seeds with a note that says, "Let us help you grow your business." These are much more expensive, but more likely to be noticed.

Layer 4 advertising can provide a nice addition to the advertising you already do, or it can serve as your only form of advertising—to keep your name out there when you don't need the constant voice in the market created by CCF. Magazines, newspapers, and direct mail all serve as a way to occasionally remind your audience that you're there.

THE ROLE OF DIRECTORIES

Advertising is meant to persuade someone to act and seek you out. It is a way to encourage and persuade your audience to take a step toward you by showing them what you can do for them and getting them interested in learning more. A directory, on the other hand, is much more passive—you wait to be found. So, although advertisers (business owners like you) tend to lump directories into their discussions of advertising, these directories actually serve a very different purpose.

Directories, like the Yellow Pages or Google My Business, offer options to list your business and contact information along with other businesses in your category. Because directories are often part of the consideration when it comes to advertising budgets, we'll cover it here. However, they don't apply to any of the layers in the advertising toolbox because they are not really advertising.

Media advertising is *active* and directories are *passive*; advertising causes you to be *sought*, directories make sure you can be *found*.

Putting most of your focus in active advertising means that more customers will want to do business with you and will go to the directory for your phone number only. Even if they see the entire list of businesses in your category, you stand a better chance of being *picked* because the person searching is familiar with you.

HARDCOPY DIRECTORIES

Ah the Yellow Pages. Ask anyone under 35 where they keep their phone book and they'll say "huh?" Why? Because Google! But although they are becoming less and less popular and most communities are scaling back home delivery or cancelling it altogether, they are still being printed.

Note that not all communities will have hardcopy directories available, so if this does not apply to you, skip down to online directories.

STRENGTHS

Although these printed directories are an endangered species, as long as they are still around, some business owners will spend money to be included in them. Here's why:

- The Yellow Pages allows you to be found by customers who are looking for your services, especially when they don't have any specific business in mind for what they need. You have a chance to be chosen even though you haven't reached them any other way.

- An ad in the Yellow Pages can bring in business from travelers visiting your town. There is likely a directory in their hotel room, so being listed means you have a chance of getting their business.

- Restaurants that offer takeout still hang on to their Yellow Pages advertising because of the opportunity to display their menu, and because people still use the directory to order food.

- If you are targeting an older demographic, this is a valid option as older individuals are more inclined to use the phone book to find businesses. If you're targeting seniors, there is a good reason to buy a Yellow Pages ad.

LIMITATIONS

Despite the few instances that can be worthwhile, hardcopy directories are overall not worth putting in a significant amount of time, money, or effort. Older businesses still sometimes hang on to their spot simply because of the tradition of being listed in the book. If you are listed, here are a few reasons you might want to reconsider:

- Many long-time advertisers in the phone book continue spending money because of the fear of loss and because it's what they've always done. They are told by the directory advertising reps that they could lose their third-place spot in their category if they downgrade or cancel their advertising. But what good is a third-place spot in a book that is closed 99.9% of the time?

- Yellow Pages advertising gets very expensive, especially when you're paying to be listed in multiple categories. How much more effective would your advertising be if you spent that money on intrusive advertising that goes out and finds your customers instead?

  Restaurants that can't let go of printing their menu in the Yellow Pages could consider putting their menu on their website instead and using the Yellow Pages ad to invite people to go online to check out their menu or order directly online (significantly reducing the size and cost of your phonebook ad).

- Just like being in the paper, when you're in the Yellow Pages, you are literally listed next to all of your competitors. And you're hoping to be picked because of nothing more than the stock photo and headline.

- More and more, print directories are being banned or eliminated due to low usage, concerns for the environment, and recycling costs. Because there are more easily accessible online options, the phonebook is dying out.

If you are still struggling to get out of the phonebook for fear of losing your placement or missing out on potential customers, consider this: would McDonald's or Walmart ever have a full-page ad in the Yellow Pages? I don't think so. And they seem to be doing okay for themselves.

How to use them

For most business categories, if you just *have* to be listed, I would suggest that a simple (free) name and number listing is all you need if you're doing a good job marketing yourself in active media. Or at most a business card-sized ad. Consider that if you're branding yourself well, people will just look up your name in the white pages, or more likely online, instead of weeding through the Yellow Pages to find you.

Many professional service providers who have very strict regulations surrounding advertising in their category (like chiropractors and lawyers) like to be in the phone book because it is safe and doesn't put them too "out there." If you fall into this category, a print directory might be a good option, but online directories are much more widely used. If you can get a free (or relatively inexpensive) listing online, it may be your better choice.

ONLINE DIRECTORIES

These days, online directories are a much bigger player than any print directory. New directory websites pop up all the time—ones for home design, better businesses, best restaurants, and anything else you can imagine. If you're a flooring store, you may be tempted to commit to a home renovations directory. If you're a restaurant, you may want to be listed in a dining directory. Google My Business is also considered a directory.

The value and benefit of being listed in these places comes down to how much they're visited, and how much they're visited is determined by how popular they are or how much marketing is done to promote them.

STRENGTHS

Being listed in a very popular and trusted directory is a good way to be found when you're needed. The most popular, of course, is Google My Business. That's the display that shows up at the top right of Google Search results when someone searches for a business name. Google My Business applies to pretty much any business, especially those with physical stores, and can include information about opening hours, location, contact information, reviews, and even popular and busy times.

A lot of popular directories feature reviews posted by customers. When we travel, we use Yelp and TripAdvisor to source out our food and shopping. The ones that have really good reviews, or a good presence on the platform along with a menu and pictures of their food end up being the ones that we're likely to pick. Yelp and TripAdvisor are both very widely utilized and trusted directories that people use to make purchase decisions. A listing with good reviews from customers could be beneficial for your business and give you a much better chance of being picked among everyone else in the category.

LIMITATIONS

However, as I mentioned, directories are only as strong as the number of visitors they have and there are so many that are worth nothing because nobody uses them. Before you decide which ones you want to put your time and money into, find out how much traffic they get and ask a few people you know if they've heard of it.

Directories are passive vehicles, not active ones, so the same challenges apply to these as to the Yellow Pages. If you aren't branded in the mind of the searcher all you can do is hope you are chosen out of those on the list—and it is not a tool for keeping your business top-of-mind.

HOW TO USE THEM

For online directories, at the very least, you should be listed (with updated information!) on Google My Business. It's free and doesn't take too long to set up. Once it's set up, there are options to access data on how many people are searching and finding you, you can view customer reviews, and you can include photos and video of your business.

Free directories really can't hurt if they don't take too much time to set up. But when you're making the decision to be on any other one, consider the following:

- How does this directory advertise to drive traffic to their site? Do they run TV or radio ads? Do they have billboards or run Facebook ads? Do they have a dominant presence online and show up at the top of category search results? How actively are they trying to recruit customers to their site so you can be found there?

- Is the site locally focused or is it lumping everyone together from across the country? If you are the only flooring store from Toronto listed with a scattered group of interior decorating businesses from across the country, how many people in your local trading area are likely to utilize this particular directory? And how much of that website's marketing efforts are going to reach your local customers?

Skip the Dishes is a good example of a directory that is doing well. It is a Western Canada-based online hub for restaurants where you can order takeout and delivery from dozens of local and chain restaurants. Any restaurant offering takeout or delivery in the city wants to be on there because it is now the go-to place for ordering delivery in many markets. Skip the Dishes makes sure each participating restaurant displays on-site signage and window stickers for the website and the company uses broadcast media to promote the service as well.

VIDEO

When it comes to advertising, there is really no limit to what you *can* do. What you *should* do, however, is limited by your budget and by where your customers can be found. Regardless of which layer you are working in with your advertising, you want to make the most impact within your chosen activities. One recently popular option is to incorporate video into your online presence.

Video makes up about half of all mobile web traffic these days. People tend to spend more time with video posts than with text, and videos are generally more noticed and shared. People are watching everything from happy dog videos to bloopers to two-hour podcasts. They add a personality to your brand and help build trust among potential customers.

Video is becoming so popular because it draws us in and makes a memorable impression. Links are opened more often if they have video and they even improve your SEO. Recently, livestream video has become popular among advertisers—customers can watch your broadcast live or catch it later, so it's an impactful way to get attention and showcase a new product or an event.

But, why are they so effective? People are time-starved and would rather watch a video than read a lengthy article. But more importantly, we are engaged with sight and sound. Does this sound familiar? It's sight, sound, and motion, just like TV, so it's no surprise that video is being praised as the most effective content online. What the internet had been missing with advertising until the video trend emerged is the intrusive nature of sound that was working for advertisers on TV and radio.

HOW TO INTEGRATE VIDEO INTO YOUR ONLINE STRATEGY

Online marketing consultants advise their clients to use video whenever possible on their websites and share shorter clips on social media posts. Some businesses even start their own YouTube channel. Basically, any time you can add this intrusive messaging to your platforms, you'll make a stronger impression.

For your website, make sure you include high-quality video or it will reflect badly on your brand. You may want to hire a video production company or talented online marketing firm to produce something that will last. If you're creating the video content yourself, it's a good idea to invest in quality equipment like microphones and an HD camera at the very least. With social media and streaming video, although it is meant to be more casual and immediate, don't wing it. Make sure to plan and rehearse your program before going on the air.

• • •

Employing elements of each layer of advertising to draw on their unique benefits would be your ideal marketing plan. The reality is that you probably don't have a budget high enough to reach into every basket, and that isn't a bad thing. If you focus your time and money on one or two advertising vehicles that accomplish the objectives you are looking for with a big enough audience to grow your business, you will be successful. Do a really good job of those and don't worry about everything else.

Once you figure out where your audience is and you know which media you want to advertise in, getting your advertising campaign started is much less complicated than you once thought.

As we already know, there is a worldwide misperception that all forms of traditional advertising are dead and that the only options to consider are online. People are fond of saying things like, "I don't ever see any ads," or, "I'm not affected by advertising," or, "I don't listen to radio." Based on this information, millions of small businesses are moving all their marketing eggs into the online basket, then wondering why they're not getting the results they were expecting. Though we can measure reaction to online activities easier than to mass media, we can clearly see the difference in reach and exposure between online and traditional media when the two are measured back to back. The following is an interesting example of comparing apples to apples.

There is an online job search and recruitment company in the Canadian prairies called JobShop.ca. They host sites like SaskatoonJobShop.ca, ReginaJobShop.ca, CalgaryJobShop.ca, among others. They run a high frequency of commercials each week, 52 weeks of the year on a few local radio stations in each of the markets they are in—and that is their only form of advertising.[32]

I like to use JobShop as a test when I'm talking to somebody local who says, "I don't listen to radio." When I ask them if they've heard of JobShop, every single one of them is quite familiar with the company. Again, they could only have heard about the company on the radio, so while most people might think they are unaffected by advertising, that is simply not true.

Google's sales team had been targeting JobShop, asking them to move their advertising budget away from radio and into paid search. In Calgary, they finally decided to do a trial. They took all their advertising off the radio and put that money into Google AdWords. At the end of the trial period, their monthly Google traffic for the keyphrase "Calgary jobs" was 14,800; for "jobs in Calgary," it was 12,100 and for "Calgary job bank," it was 1,900. Compare this to the monthly radio reach they were getting of 137,700 people reached one time, 42,400 reached three times, and 26,900 reached five times.

The sheer number of people that they reach using radio compared to paid search with the same budget is outrageous. And they're an online-only company. That's the same reason those online travel sites turn to traditional media to reach the masses. It is simply more effective per dollar spent.

When it comes to your advertising, a good place to start is to focus on developing an excellent Layer 1 campaign, and once you've taken care of that, add in what you need from the other layers. Try not to jump into everything all at once and your advertising journey will be much easier to manage. However, that won't be the right thing for everyone. In some cases, you can rely on only online ads or magazine and newspaper ads. What will work for you will depend on your specific advertising goals, your budget, and the business you already generate from existing customers, word of mouth, and your storefront.

In Chapter 6, we'll get into the details of setting up your campaign and setting a budget that matches your goals. For now, consider these questions:

HOMEWORK

1. Which layers of advertising have you covered with your marketing so far?

   a. Where are you achieving consistency (C)?

   b. Where are you sending a creative, compelling message (C)?

   c. Where are you achieving frequency (F)?

2. How much of your effort is put into active advertising (being sought)? How much of it is passive (waiting to be found)?

3. Which two tools can you use with consistency *and* frequency to speak to your chosen audience?

CHAPTER 6

Buying Ads

"Doing business without advertising is like winking at a girl in the dark. You know what you are doing, but nobody else does."

— Stewart Henderson Britt

As we already know, there are countless options available to you when it comes to advertising your business. It can be overwhelming even now that you understand the foundations of advertising.

In this chapter, we'll dig into how you can choose the advertising media you'll use and how to determine how much money you should spend to get the results you're looking for. We'll be referring to the advertising layers concept from Chapter 5, so you'll want to review that before moving on.

Let's dig into your options a little further and work through some exercises to help customize the media selection for your business.

How to buy

Buying advertising can be a daunting task—which media should you choose? How will you get your ads written? Who should you advertise to? These are all great questions and this section is designed to help you figure out the answers for yourself.

Pick a medium and own it

In advertising, there are dozens of balloons floating in the air; dozens of opportunities to reach an audience with your ad message. It would be impossible to catch them all. How do you decide which ones to focus on and grab ahold of?

When I'm talking to a business owner for the first time, most just don't know where to start with their advertising. There are so many balloons to choose from—they see so many markets they could cater to and focus on, so they often they find themselves just reacting to whatever comes their way and feeling like they have no plan.

Advertising doesn't have to be like that for you. Your business doesn't have to be everywhere and it doesn't have to be everything for everyone. As you've probably figured out by now, you have to know what you stand for and how you want to serve your customers before you can start branding yourself and advertising effectively. But what do you do once you've narrowed that down? Your customer base is going to be made up of lots of different types of people who consume many different types of media, so how do you know where to start?

Some advertising salespeople have probably told you to spread out your advertising budget by purchasing a little bit of everything. That is bad advice and they are likely telling you that so their product is included in your purchase decision, not because it's the best thing for your business. Instead, start by picking one medium and owning it. That's all you need to do. Just pick one medium. Within any reasonably sized media audience, there will be many people who will do business with you or who know people who will do business with you.

Ask yourself this question: is it better to reach 100% of the population and convince them 10% of the way, or to reach 10% of the population and convince them 100% of the way?

You could spend your entire budget—a little bit in each of a number of media—and, by the end of the year, have nothing to show for it because you spread yourself too thin. Or, you could completely own one audience and become a household name with them by the end of the year. You are better off choosing one thing and sticking with it until they can't help but think of you when they need you, than just doing a little of this and a little of that.

Figure out the size of audience that you can afford to reach and do it all the time. Commit to communicating with one audience on an ongoing basis, even if it's a small one. Only add other media as your business grows and you have more budget to spend. Note that once you start advertising on one medium, representatives from other media will start calling on you to buy their products. It is tempting to jump around between the different options, but it's important to not be led astray! Keep those other good ideas in mind for when you're ready to *add* to what you're already doing.

Choosing the "right" people

It can be tempting to over-analyze your audience. It is important to target a very specific group if you have a small marketing budget—especially online. However, more often than not, over-targeted campaigns do not work as well as broad ones that cast a bigger net.

By saying, "The target for my bakery is a woman 35–50 years old from a dual-income household with a couple of kids, so that's the only demographic I'm targeting with my advertising," you're basically saying that nobody else is worth your advertising dollar—not her husband, her kids, her parents, or anyone else that might buy cake. I mean seriously, *it's cake!! Who doesn't like cake?!*

Proctor & Gamble (P&G), the biggest advertiser in the world, recently concluded that their decision to target only specific demographics on Facebook narrowed their reach too much and was a mistake. For instance, two years ago they targeted their Facebook ads for Febreze (a household air freshener) to pet owners and households with large families. Sales of Febreze stagnated. Then, when they expanded their reach to everyone over 18 years of age on social media *and* TV, their sales grew. P&G has started shifting their spending back into television advertising and is seeing great results. Because they are now reaching their target *and* influencers, they are able to make a larger overall impact, which drives more sales.

So, don't worry too much about reaching only the exact right audience with your advertisements. Yes, you want to know who your target is because you want your ads to address their needs and wants, but you don't want to narrow your focus too much when it comes to spreading that message.

As social beings, we all have influencers around us—250 people who would be at your wedding and 250 people who would be at your funeral. When you're in the market for a new product or service and don't have a business in mind, chances are you ask around for recommendations. You'll ask people who to call if you need a plumber or an electrician, where they shop for furniture, and what they think of the new Italian restaurant. Your purchase decision might be made because of the combination of hearing an ad on the radio and a mention from a friend.

When it comes to advertising, we tend to forget that our target should not necessarily be limited to the people who will be using the product. Men's clothing stores advertise to women because they know that a wife is often the one who takes her husband shopping because he looks like a hobo (not speaking from personal experience here or anything). So, with your advertising, it is not a bad thing to reach not only your potential client, but also people who *know* your client. Don't assume the only value is in reaching men who are buying clothes. Consider that reaching their wives and girlfriends and moms who will take them shopping—or at least tell them where to go—is also valuable. *Everyone you reach is a customer or knows one.*

The impact of your ad campaigns won't be only because of reaching your ideal customer but also their influencers.

While you don't have to target those influencers specifically, expanding your pool to one that includes them can have a positive impact on your advertising success. While you might save a few dollars on a Facebook ad by targeting a small group, you won't be reaching other people who help buyers make their decisions, meaning you are limiting your potential overall impact.

Though we don't want to over-target and be too narrow in our reach, we also need to be careful not to try to reach too many people.

REACHING TOO MANY PEOPLE

One of the biggest mistakes people make in advertising is trying to reach too many people with too little budget. There are a couple of ways to make this mistake:

1. The advertiser **buys a big campaign and spends all their money in a short amount of time** (1–3 months or a few weeks here and there), then goes the rest of the year without any ads at all because they have no more money to spend.

   They pay to reach a large audience in a short time, but what if many of those people don't need their product right now? Will they still remember the business in nine months? Not likely, considering how many other ad messages they'll hear in that time. It's better to reach fewer people (make a smaller splash), but keep your communication with that group consistent throughout the year. You have a much better chance of getting into their long-term memory and being top-of-mind when the need arises if you keep your campaign going longer.

2. The advertiser **buys a media mix with a little bit of advertising in a lot of different media.** The business ends up with a tiny presence on a couple of radio stations, in the community newspaper, on a billboard periodically, and every few weeks they pay for an ad on Facebook. They might reach a lot of people with this combination, but the number of impressions per person is much too low to make an impact on any of them.

Advertisers like to think that a single prospect will see their billboard *and* hear their radio ad *and* read the paper *and* see the Facebook ad and connect the dots. But the reality is that the audiences of those media don't overlap enough to achieve the frequency you need with each individual, and the customers do not have enough of a vested interest to try and connect all of those dots.

So, if you shouldn't spend your whole budget on a wide reach for a few months, or by mixing light media coverage over a longer period of time, what is a more effective strategy? Well, since consistency and frequency are key, they should be your priorities. Fit your campaign into your budget and focus on reaching only the size of audience you can afford to reach on a year-round basis. For example, if you're buying radio and you don't have the budget for a dominant presence morning, afternoon, and evening all year, you can go even smaller by limiting the timeslots you advertise in so you only own a portion of that listening audience.

As your business grows, you can add to the size of audience you're reaching by adding on more timeslots, more stations, and eventually other layers. When you do this, don't abandon the original audience if the advertising has been working for you. Instead, build on what you have already established and keep giving your original audience the chance to accept your invitation when they need you. For example, if you started with one radio station, there are still many listeners who know about you but simply haven't needed you yet.

When Brainsport started their advertising, they chose to target the weekend listening audience on the pop radio station first. Then, when they wanted to increase their reach, instead of moving on to a different station or a different medium altogether, they simply added weekday commercials and extra frequency onto what they were already doing. As Brainsport spoke to the pop station audience over the course of 15 years, listeners became adults, had babies, took up running, needed better shoes, and had kids who joined track and field. These developments are happening all the time within any one target group, so because they stuck with that original audience, they saw thousands of new faces walk through their doors every year, all from that same listening audience. They didn't expect everyone to just remember an ad campaign they ran 15 years ago. They simply committed to their audience, reminding them of who they are and what they do, knowing that eventually, when those pop listeners needed new shoes, they would think of Brainsport, because they had been hearing their message for so long.

This is the key: long-term, frequent, and consistent messaging.

Selecting your media

Now that you have an idea of how the long-term advertising game works, let's review the layers and figure out which media you should work on. In this section, take some time to answer the questions posed. They'll help you work toward determining the right path. For this exercise we will once again refer to our Advertising Toolbox:

Where you exist

Where you exist is based on your physical location and your website. Here are the things you might consider when deciding whether to invest some advertising dollars into where you exist:

Your physical location

Does your signage need an upgrade? Is it easy to read, high quality, and bright? Or is it worn out or cracked? Maybe it no longer reflects the brand elements (colors, logo, etc.) you have developed since you opened. You may want to spend some money upgrading that before you move on.

YOUR WEBSITE

Does your site look like it was created in the 90s? Does it say, "Last updated April 2012?" You should make sure that you are putting your best foot forward on your website. Hire someone to build a site for you or spend some time creating a good one on WordPress or another site-building platform. And don't forget to make sure it's mobile optimized.

THE BASELINE

Word of mouth and social media (a.k.a. word of mouth on steroids) is key. Think about what you are doing to take advantage of the positive word of mouth that is happening, or if there is more you should be doing here.

WORD OF MOUTH

Are you making your customers happy and providing a positive and memorable experience? If so, are you asking your happy customers to give you referrals? Guess what. This is free!

SOCIAL MEDIA

Are you already on social media? If so, where? How much engagement do you get? What is your cost per impression? Are you managing it well or does it need some improvement? Is the time you're putting in worth the results you're getting?

If you aren't already on social media, or you know you need to take the leap, start by deciding which social media platforms are right for your business based on where your customers are and what you are comfortable and confident using. Figure out where your customers are by spending some time on each platform and observing where they are hanging out. Keep in mind that not all businesses are suitable for social media.

Facebook is by far the most dominant social media platform in the world, with 1.8 billion active users across the globe, compared to Instagram at 600 million, Tumblr at 550 million, Twitter at 317 million, and Pinterest and LinkedIn both at less than 200 million.[1] Facebook has a strong presence across all age groups from 16 to 64 years old—though there is a perception that Facebook is for older people, the largest group of Facebook users is 18–29 years old, followed by 30–49-year-olds. Instagram, YouTube, and Twitter users are relatively spread out among age groups, while Snapchat and Kik are used primarily by 16–24-year-olds followed by 25–34-year-olds.[2]

Just like any other marketing decision, choose the platform(s) you'll use and be consistent. If you can only do one thing well, that is better than doing a few things poorly. Keep in mind that Facebook and Twitter are primarily "pay to play" platforms now, so your free posts will not likely reach your audience.

If you choose more than one social networking platform for your business, you can make it easy on yourself by using a social media dashboard like Hootsuite, Sprout Social, or Buffer. These are services that allow you to post on multiple social media networks at once, monitor trends and conversations, respond to feedback, and schedule your messages, all from one dashboard.

LAYER 1: THE FOUNDATION

Your foundation, where you can best achieve CCF, is broadcast media, like radio and TV. They establish the base layer of brand-building.

Before you make any decisions about which medium is right for you or which stations you want to advertise on, meet with a couple of sales reps from your local stations to find out more about their audience and how much you'll have to spend. We call this layer the foundation because advertising with *sound* is what will get you into the long-term memory of your audience and build you into a household name.

RADIO

When speaking with media reps, find out how much it would cost to reach their entire listening audience to achieve a frequency of three with any given listener. This usually means running 21–25 full-day rotation commercials per week.

If your budget does not allow you to run this many ads on the station, find out how you can build dominance by buying "a station within a station." This means that you run ads consistently at the same time each day, or the same day(s) each week. Becoming the sponsor of the morning news, where you receive a name credit and a 30-second commercial every morning at the same time, is a good example of this. You are not reaching the station's whole audience, but you are building CCF with those who tend to listen at that time.

Most radio listeners listen to radio at the same times each day and on the same days each week out of habit and routine. Some radio stations offer weekend packages or evening schedules, which are other ways that you can have a consistent presence year-round without spreading yourself too thin.

Note that media reps often try to offer a schedule that reaches as many people as possible, but it can come at the expense of reaching individual listeners with frequency. A reduced schedule with more frequency aimed at a smaller segment of the audience is your better bet. Don't get caught up in conversations about statistics and ratings; what you want to do is buy a schedule that achieves CCF with the size of audience your budget is suited to. One of our radio stations ran commercials for a burger joint in their all-night show because that's the only schedule the restaurant could afford. The restaurant was not open at night, but there were plenty of shift workers and night owls who heard from them night after night, so the campaign was a huge success.

If you cannot afford a "station within a station," consider looking at a smaller (less popular) radio station in your market or fill the year as consistently as you can on your chosen station with six- or eight-week runs taking short breaks in between.

TELEVISION

When speaking with TV reps, ask them how you can place your commercials so that the same viewer is likely to see your ad at least three times in seven-nights' sleep. This may mean sponsoring the morning or evening news or buying ads targeted at a specific demographic in primetime programming (the demographics of viewers on network TV tends to change throughout the day). People don't watch one TV channel all day long, every day, so you need to be more strategic in how your ads are placed if you want to reach the same person with frequency. It's tricky and can be expensive to hit the same person two or three times weekly, but if you can make it work, TV will have a lot of impact.

Besides local network stations, you can buy specialty cable channels that reach a specific demographic that may match your target audience, like home and garden or DIY channels. You can also buy ads in specific geographic zones on cable channels, so you don't end up advertising on the other side of the country for your local small business. And there is an emerging opportunity to buy ads on the online version of the TV channel and in TV on-demand.

SEARCH ENGINE OPTIMIZATION

While building your brand in the market using radio or TV to become specifically *sought*, you should simultaneously be putting some effort into ensuring that you can be *found* online when customers search your category. Talk to a reputable web marketing firm who can implement some strategies to get you on the first page of the Google search results list. Remember, if your category only has a handful of businesses in it, there is no need to pay for SEO as you will appear on the first page of search results automatically.

SEO dominance is an ever-changing game as Google updates its algorithms and criteria for organic search result success, and these web marketing firms will keep on top of the trends and adapt your strategy as they need to. But keep in mind that being found in your general category is not as important as branding your name so that people come looking for you. Less of your effort and budget should be going toward SEO and more should be going to intrusive branding. Some experts suggest it should be a 25/75 split (SEO/intrusive branding). If you meet with an online marketing firm who doesn't understand that there needs to be a balance and suggest that all of your budget should go to SEO, they may not be the best firm to help you achieve your goals.

LAYER 2: FREQUENCY

Layer 2 focuses on outdoor ads and paid online options to increase your frequency and remind your audience what you can do for them.

You'll know you're ready for Layer 2 when:

a)   You have booked your 52-week campaign on radio or TV and still have money for extra frequency, or

b)   You do not have a big enough budget or need for a Layer 1 medium, or

c)   You have a simple call to action or can grab enough interest and attention with a few words and a compelling image (like a clothing store featuring an outfit and a brand name).

OUTDOOR

Your billboards, bus wraps, bench ads, and digital signs offer the opportunity to make frequent impressions on the market. A few ways to approach outdoor advertising are:

- Pick a high-traffic location and own the billboard space—move it a few times a year.

- Blanket your business's neighborhood with billboards, bus bench ads, and digital signs.

- Buy a frequency campaign on public transit to be seen with repetition in all the areas of town that those vehicles go.

For your outdoor ads, have a simple call to action and an image that gets noticed, or include a small part of the message you are sending through radio or TV and use your outdoor ads as a reminder of the bigger story you're telling through sound.

PAID ONLINE ADVERTISING

If you don't have the budget to cast a big net and reach the masses, targeted online advertising is a good way to reach your people. Make the best of your limited budget by:

- Speaking to them consistently. If this is your only form of advertising, make sure your audience is seeing an ad at least two or three times a week. If it is a complement to mass media advertising, then less often is okay.

- Giving them a reason to remember you or click through for more information.

- Incorporating video wherever you can to increase your click-through rate and add movement and sound to your message.

There are online marketing companies who can do a good job of this for you if you are not inclined to do it yourself. Talk to a few of them and hire the one whose rates are reasonable and who you feel truly understands branding and how to balance being found with being sought.

LAYER 3: FOLLOW-UP COMMUNICATION

Once your location and Layers 1 and 2 are working for you and bringing in new prospects, use social media and newsletters to continue the relationship. It's easier to keep happy customers coming back than to gain new customers, so adding your customers to your newsletter mailing list and encouraging them to follow you on social media are easy and almost free ways to remind them to shop you again and more often.

Some steps you can take to build an effective follow-up strategy include:

- Train and remind your staff to ask each customer at the checkout if they are on your mailing list/email database (post a reminder by the till).

- Include a call to action on your website that invites visitors to join your mailing list.

- Collect social media and newsletter content by being on the lookout for interesting articles from various sources and following thought leaders in your business category. Share themost relevant content you find (and credit those sources when you include their material, of course).

- Schedule time each month to compile the content you've collected into a newsletter and schedule your upcoming social media posts. You could also designate a staff member to do this or hire a third-party social media management company.

- Decide if you want to find or purchase content for newsletters. If you purchase, your only job is to put it all together and send it out.

Whatever you decide to do, make sure to set up a system that will ensure you keep up with it.

LAYER 4: EXTRA BLASTS

Your extra blasts form the fourth layer of advertising. These include advertising in magazines and newspapers and your direct mail campaigns. While they likely won't be your primary advertising media to build your brand, these extra blasts can offer a nice boost to your voice when your budget allows.

MAGAZINES AND NEWSPAPERS

After you have implemented Layers 1, 2, and/or 3, or have chosen to skip them, you can consider newspaper and magazine ads as feature pieces. If you've gotten to this point, here are two questions to consider that will help determine if magazine and newspaper ads are right for you:

- Is there a lifestyle or trade magazine in the area that suits your business or is specific to your business category?

- Is there a newspaper you like that you know your target audience reads (like a student newspaper at your local college)?

If there is a publication that is specific to your niche market and you know that it is well-read among your customers, running a traditional ad in that publication could be a good idea, especially if you can afford to run it consistently. Sometimes it is the right thing to have a presence there as part of that small community. Run an ad designed to showcase your brand or your work and try to have it located near an article related to your industry if possible.

Running an advertorial (a paid ad that looks like an article) can be a way to tell people more about the story behind your business, feature your key staff members, and share more about your brand. People notice and read these articles differently than they do ads because they look like content, which is what most readers are there for. However, if you feel that you have a good story to tell, consider pitching it to the magazine editor to run as an actual story. If it's rejected, think twice about paying to print it. If it is not interesting enough to be published as a story, then people likely won't want to read it if you've paid to publish it.

If you don't have a big budget, print ads and especially advertorials may not be right for you as they can be cost prohibitive for a frequency of one in any given month or quarter, so look at them like I tell my kids to look at cookies—as a "sometimes food."

DIRECT MAIL

You can use flyers periodically to tell your neighborhood about something that's changed, like a new product line you're carrying or special pricing you're offering. If you just opened your business, a series of flyer drops can be a good way to introduce yourself to your surrounding neighborhoods.

GETTING FREE ADVERTISING

Although your main focus should be on your paid advertising campaigns, look for opportunities to get some free advertising to enhance your presence in the market. Don't consider free advertising as a replacement for your paid advertising—it isn't enough to get your message out there consistently and frequently—but do consider these often under-utilized options to enhance your messaging.

TV & RADIO

Often, the TV and radio partners you already work with can provide some free exposure for you in a couple of ways.

CONTESTS

Most TV and radio stations do regular prize giveaways—sometimes daily, other times weekly—or prizing tied into bigger contests they run. These are great opportunities to tell people about your products with more frequency and get your business' name out there. In fact, aligning yourself with a reputable station helps position you in the market, and research has shown that product placement in contests like these adds credibility to the product you're featuring.[3]

Don't expect to get in on these contests completely without any cash commitment (unless it's a very small station with a shortage of prizes, in which case, go for it!), but if you are a current advertiser with the station or purchase a certain volume of advertising to be part of the promotion, there will be opportunities for you to be included. By being part of a contest you will be included in extra live mentions, recorded promotional messages, and content on the station's websites and social posts that is often worth thousands more than the advertising you have purchased.

Think about it—stations run these promotions to get more listeners to listen more often, so they are *all over* these contests. They promote the heck out of them because it is in their best interest. Why would you *not* want to include your business name in that extra buzz—especially if you were going to pay to be on the station anyway?

If you don't sell products or services that are appropriate as prize giveaways, you can sometimes still be part of a contest by providing a cash prize, or by sponsoring a prize that has mass appeal, like a fuel gift card or an iPad.

MORNING SHOWS

As TV is becoming a more and more national medium, local channels have brought a portion of their programming back to the local market by hosting engaging morning shows. They are always looking for quality local content, and that provides a unique opportunity to feature your business. You can appear on a morning show to do a demo of your service, display the fall lineup of your products, educate viewers on a topic related to your industry, or tell the city about an upcoming event.

Not only do you appear on the show, but you can then share your appearance online and have your friends re-share it. Note that some stations charge you to be on the show and others do not, but if your story is deemed by the station to be newsworthy and relevant to the audience, you may get featured at no cost to you.

COMMUNITY EVENT ANNOUNCEMENTS

If you run a regular charity or community event, or are tied in with a non-profit initiative, see what kind of coverage you can get through community event messages. Again your main motivation should be to give back to the community and not just for the publicity, but it will end up benefiting both the charity and your business if you raise awareness about the work you are doing. Send out a short, concise press release to all the media in your area making clear what the event is, who it is helping, that your business is involved, and most importantly, why it's newsworthy. This will serve to help the initiative get more coverage and you'll get credit for being the sponsor.

Most local newspapers list community events and often write feature articles about those events. Most radio and television stations run 'around town' messages on air. Getting yourself included in these can bring in a bigger crowd to your event and can reaffirm your association to the charity.

If you are an advertiser with any of the media you are sending the press release to, also send it to your advertising rep and ask them to pass it along to the promotions department. The media receive hundreds of press releases each week, so do whatever you can to not get lost in the pile.

EVENT CALENDARS

Since you're likely already working with media partners and those partners probably have community event listings on their websites, ask to have yours included as well. Whenever you run an event, let your media partners know and have them include your event in their online listings. They invite their viewers and listeners to their websites all day, every day, so being on their website is another way to make an impression on their audience.

BRIBERY

Okay, you didn't hear this from me, but why not gift some local celebrities, media personalities, and influencers a sample basket of your products? Now, they're not officially (usually) allowed to accept gifts, but if a well-intended gift makes it to them, they will either mention it on air or find some opportunity to give you a shout-out among their followers.

If you are inclined to provide a gift like this, focus your efforts on personalities you already have a working relationship with—they are more likely to help you out.

PRINT MEDIA

Although print is less dominant these days, posters and community newspapers are still widely seen. If you're running an event in the area, these are ways to add a little boost to your turnout and encourage more people to show up to your store.

COMMUNITY NEWSPAPERS

Look for community newspapers that have a regular "new business" feature. If you are a new business (or an existing business offering something new and newsworthy), try to get yourself listed and you may even get an article written about you. Since people notice and read articles differently than ads, it can be an effective way to raise awareness about what you are doing and drive traffic to your store.

GOOD OL' POSTERS

People still walk down the street and hang out at coffee shops. If you have a small budget to print posters, have your teenage kids (or pay your friends' kids) to poster the area when something special is happening at your store. If you're running a sale or promotion or if you're having a community or in-store event, put together a simple poster to get the word out.

EVENTS AND IN-STORE

Getting noticed comes in many forms from the most obvious (standing outside waving "look at me!" to passersby) to the subtler (having an emcee wear your product on stage).

These are tactics that remind people about your business and show support for your community.

EMBARRASS YOUR STAFF

Your location is one of the baseline layers of your advertising, so what better way to get people to notice you than to make sure you stand out at your own location?

There is a flower shop in our city that has had teenaged staff members out in front of their store for *years*, waving at cars as they drive by while holding a sign saying something like, "Make her day. Bring home a bouquet!" or "In the doghouse? Stop in for flowers." I *hope* the same teenager hasn't been there the whole time (haha), but what a great way to keep a staff member busy on a slow day!

My father-in-law who owns a couple of Dairy Queen restaurants (did I mention I married for free ice cream?) has half-jokingly asked us to stand out front dressed in a huge, creepy DQ ice cream cone costume and wave to traffic. I have a feeling that now that our kids are almost old enough to start working there, the costume may come out again. But for now, thankfully, it's harboring mothballs in grandpa's backyard shed.

Although it may sound like a joke, having someone hold a sign or dress up in a costume outside your store draws attention and reminds people you're there. If you're located in a busy area, consider what you could do to stand out from everyone else around you.

PRODUCT PLACEMENT

If you're a dress shop, outfit the person who emcees the biggest events. If you are a restaurant, cater events where media broadcast live. Think of ways that you can get your product in front of crowds while at the same time helping to make the event better. Be creative. Think of where your customers are and how you may be able to get them to try your product.

SUPPORT A COMMUNITY CAUSE OR CHARITY

A commitment to consistently support one or two causes in your community will lead to good PR and top-of-mind awareness among the group that is benefiting from your support as well as the general public. Here are some ways you can support your community:

- Host or organize an annual event
- Donate gift certificates or products as door prizes or silent auction items
- Go with your staff to volunteer at the food bank, a Habitat for Humanity build, or charity Christmas gift wrapping
- Give a cash donation
- Donate the use of your facility as a gathering space to non-profit organizations

Business owners want to give back to the community that supports them, so it is good practice to get involved. Though your main motivation should not be for the press it gets you, raising your profile in a positive way in the community will be a happy by-product of your efforts.

RUNNING PROMOTIONS AND SALES

Throughout this book, we've focused on branding and building your messaging and media coverage so you can tell everyone in your market about who you are and what you do. We've explored the different tools available to you and how each of them can make impressions on customers to achieve ongoing top-of-mind awareness.

However, I haven't mentioned special offers, promotions, limited time offers, or sale events. Though that's not the focus of this book and should not be the focus of the bulk of your advertising, it still deserves a mention because when used properly, special event advertising can be a useful tool in your marketing.

Some ways that you can use a limited time offer in your marketing plan, include:

GRAND OPENING EVENT

Drive immediate traffic to your door, so people see what you are about shortly after you open. You can hold a grand opening event with special pricing, gifts with purchase, draws, free burgers, balloons, product demonstrations, and free samples. This can be an excellent way to kick off your business on a positive note. For best results, wait until a few weeks after you open so you can work out all the major customer service and product kinks before inviting crowds to break down your door.

I recall a restaurant in our city that had the radio station broadcast live from their restaurant the day they opened. The kitchen and front staff were not prepared for the volume of orders they got from the crowd lined up outside. As a result, the food was not prepared as well as it should have been and wait times were very long. Unfortunately, that restaurant started out with a very bad first impression and it took them a long time to recover and change their reputation. Avoid this same fate by working out the issues *before* the event.

YEARLY CUSTOMER APPRECIATION EVENT

You can hold an event with special pricing every year or a couple of times a year to get new people to try you for a lower price. For existing customers, it's an opportunity for you to give back or "wow" them.

INVENTORY CLEARANCE OR END-OF-SEASON SALE

If you're a seasonal business, you likely change your stock around several times a year. A way to get rid of old stock or anything that didn't sell well at regular price is to offer an end-of-season sale or inventory clearance event. You bring in new customers *and* make room for new products.

SPECIAL SHOPPING EVENT

Get a kick start on your key seasons with a special shopping party for your loyal customers. If you're a gift shop, have a Christmas shopping night in early November to get people in the mood to shop for the season and make them more likely to get their gifts from you!

If you sell seasonal products, offer an event early in the season so you're the first ones to get business in your category. If there is no season for your products, you can still host shopping events for products that people buy year-round and turn it into an annual thing.

DEMO DAYS

If you sell products that have unique features or something different to offer, invite your supplier reps in to demonstrate your product lines or sample food items. This will give customers exposure to products that they may not notice when they're normally shopping. It's a way to showcase new products you carry or remind people of additional ways they can use the products you offer.

CROSS-PROMOTIONS

A cross-promotion event is one where you work with community partners or other businesses to host an event. This can be a fundraiser for a charity or special interest group or a pop-up shop that showcases a number of participating businesses for a short amount of time. By combining efforts, all businesses involved get more exposure by drawing from, and combining, all of their groups of followers. Besides cross-promotional events, you can also partner with a complimentary business for an ongoing cross-promotion where you include a gift or coupon from the other store with every purchase at your store. You can pool resources to promote this benefit to your customers and it allows you to support each other and send business back and forth.

EVENT ADVERTISING

Advertising for a special event follows completely different rules than branding. With branding, you want to gradually and permanently get yourself into the long-term memory of your customers, so you need to think long-term with your advertising. But with events and promotions, you want to see quick results.

For the best chance of getting a large crowd to your event, you'll need to create a big splash over a short amount of time leading up to the event—a big newspaper ad, a strong billboard, a multi-channel blast online, a high frequency of radio ads each day, or even a live broadcast. This would be the time to advertise with a mix of media, rather than sticking to just one channel (as long as you have the budget to buy a big enough campaign on each. Otherwise stick to one and do it well).

Your event and message needs to give people a reason to stop what they're doing and head to your store right now. And a prize giveaway isn't enough to do that (usually) because few people will drop everything for a one in 500 chance of winning something. There has to be a direct cost saving or additional benefit to the customer.

Events and sales are good ways to enhance and punctuate your regular marketing efforts. However, I strongly caution you to use these sparingly and not make them a regular occurrence. You want your customers to get to know you and appreciate your worth, so they attach value to your offer and are therefore willing to pay regular price for what you sell. Your products and services build loyalty. Discounting your products too often cause long-term problems. Here's why:

- You don't want to train your audience to wait until there is a flyer or sale before coming in. Too many big retail chains have trained their audiences to not shop at full price, because there will always be another sale. For example, would you ever buy bath towels at full price at the department store? No, because you know they'll be on sale again soon.

- You want people to value your product or service at full price because you are solving a problem for them.

- The customers you gain because of a discount are just as likely to go to your competition for a better price next time—you won't build loyalty with completely price-driven customers.

- Sales are less and less effective the more often you do them. The first one seems very special to customers, but with sales happening frequently, you'll have to offer bigger and bigger discounts each time to get the same response. Think of some of the businesses in your area that are always on sale. Do you really believe that it's the biggest sale on electronics ever?

- Running too many sales turn your products and services into commodities. You open yourself up to compete against Amazon and the big online giants of the world if the only benefit you offer is price.

- Your message is forgotten the moment the event is over, so there is virtually no residual benefit or brand awareness built from the sale ads you ran.

Events and promotions are good ways to bring in new customers and show appreciation for the ones you already have, but too many promotions can backfire on you. It is reasonable to offer a couple of promotions a year, or at most one per season. This way, they are special events, not regular offerings, so customers are less likely to wait for the next sale to make a purchase and more likely to appreciate a sale when it comes.

SETTING A BUDGET

Let's face it, advertising is not cheap. No matter which free options you can take advantage of, the best way to brand yourself is through a consistent paid advertising campaign. If it's done wisely, it's an investment that should more than pay for itself and won't be a sunk cost. But exactly how much should you spend?

Your advertising budget will be one of the biggest determining factors in your advertising selections and the amount you can spend will be what dictates how many people you can afford to reach with your message. Remember, the wider the net you cast, the more people you will reach. So, determine what you can afford to spend for the year, and then divide it by 12 to get your monthly advertising budget.

A guideline to help determine how many people you can afford to reach effectively is to think of it as costing **one dollar per person per year**. So, if you have $30,000 to spend, you can consistently reach about 30,000 people in the year with your message and brand them with it—assuming your message is about average in salience.[4]

WHEN YOU'RE FIRST STARTING

In Chapter 1, I told you about the store owner who had put all her focus toward product lines and in-store experience, and neglected to set aside any money for advertising. Entrepreneurs budget for the party—rent, leasehold improvements, staff, utilities, products, and cleaning supplies—but for some reason they often don't budget (or they under-budget) for party invitations—their advertising.

When you put together your business plan, there is usually a section for marketing, and in your budget summary, a space to include your marketing budget. Typically, it is a percentage of your projected revenue. More often than not, the amount you allocate is not enough to do a good job.

Marketing experts recommend that you spend up to 20% of your gross revenue to market your business in the first few years. Of course a baby business in its first year may have to ramp up some sales before it can spend this much. If that's the case, they can just pick a set dollar amount that they feel they can afford in that first year.

This seems like a lot of money, but remember, you are starting from scratch and building brand equity in a market where nobody has ever heard of you. You need to create a voice for yourself and that doesn't happen without an investment. Getting customers through the door is the most important thing, so inviting them to do so deserves a good chunk of your budget and attention.

Like everything in life, you get what you pay for, so the more advertising you do, the more you will be giving the opportunity to respond to your message. **Marketing and advertising are not where you should be trying to scrimp and save.**

MAINTENANCE

After the first three to five years in business, once you feel like your company is starting to be known in the community, you can take your foot off the advertising pedal a bit, but you don't want to stop advertising altogether. Once you've worked so hard to build momentum, it's much easier to maintain your awareness in the market than it is to completely stop everything and build it all up again from zero. But at this point, your budget doesn't have to be quite as aggressive as it was in the first three to five years.

Experts recommend spending 4–12% of gross revenue for an ongoing maintenance campaign. As long as your business is growing, the dollar amount you are spending each year will grow with it. Many businesses set a dollar amount and then spend the exact same amount every year on their advertising. This isn't a terrible way to budget your advertising money, but when you don't increase your budget as you grow, you are not capitalizing on your increasing capacity to reach more people—especially because advertising rates go up over time, so you start to get less for your investment.

If you've been in business for a long time, when was the last time you reviewed why you spend what you spend? Have you been sticking to the same dollar amount for your marketing budget for the past 10 years even though your revenue has been growing? If so, you are missing out on a lot of potential customers by simply not taking advantage of the bigger voice you could have in the market.

Factors to consider

Although we can typically assume you will spend 4–12% of revenue per year on advertising, there are some factors that will determine if you should be at the high or low end of that range. Consider these:

- **Your location**—the farther off the beaten path you are, the more you'll need to spend to get people to your store. The more foot and road traffic in front of your store, the less advertising you need to do because you have at least some built-in visibility. Your cost of occupancy is likely higher if you're in a busier location, and you should consider that cost as part of your advertising, or more accurately, your "overall cost of exposure."

  Note: If you're in a mall, you are paying a premium to benefit from the traffic that the mall attracts. Find out if you can "piggyback" on the advertising the mall is doing, like being included in or splitting media ads or sponsoring events happening in the mall. Also, you may be able to negotiate better rates from your media source if the mall is a volume buyer of that particular medium—ask if there are mall rates that can be extended to you. Don't assume that being in the mall will be all the advertising you need. You probably will need some of your own as well.

- **Your markup**—if you're in the retail business, your markup can and should affect your exposure budget.

If your average markup is less than 100%, you will have less money to spend on advertising, so you would be on the lower end of the 4–12% of revenue going to advertising. If your markup is higher, you'll move up higher in the budget range.

- **Your product price point**—when you need to sell a high volume of products that are relatively inexpensive, you can only justify spending a few dollars for each customer you acquire. So, you need a megaphone—TV or radio—to reach the volume of people you'll need. If you are selling a premium product in the thousands of dollars, you can justify paying a salesperson to talk to your customers one-on-one and may need or use less mass marketing.

- **Your competition**—the more competitors you have, the bigger the voice you need in the market to gain market share. If you are competing with other stores that have a loud advertising voice, your campaign needs to be louder, so you get considered and shopped.

- **The size of your audience**—if you sell mass-market products with wide appeal, your audience will be much larger than if you sell specialized equipment to a relatively small group. For example, if you offer protective clothing for mine workers, your messaging will be a lot more targeted than if you sell cupcakes. That being the case, you can spend less money on your advertising by focusing on things like trade magazine advertising and targeted online ads.

- **Your current brand awareness**—if you are completely new to your area or you have been silent in your advertising for a while, you will have much less brand awareness than a business that has spent years speaking to their audience. The less known you are, the more you'll need to invest to get your name out there.

Note: Are you a franchise that is well-known? Does your franchise maintain a good presence in the market on your behalf? If so, you can probably get away with a smaller budget.

Once you figure out how much you can and will spend on advertising, it is worthwhile to consider the value of that investment when it starts gaining you customers.

AVERAGE CUSTOMER VALUE

Once you have committed to spending money, you want to know that it's worth it. Understanding the value of your average customer will help you appreciate what those marketing dollars are doing for you and help you justify the dollar amount in your mind.

To determine the lifetime value of your average client, take your average sale multiplied by how many times the same client will buy from you in a year and how many years that customer will stay with you.

Here are some examples:

- Say you're selling high-end flooring and backsplash tile. Your average customer will spend about $8000 on tiles for their home. They will obviously not build a new house multiple times a year, so you can consider this a one-time purchase. Every new person you bring in with your advertising has the potential to be worth about $8000 over their lifetime.

- If you are a hair stylist, some of your customers spend $200 per visit because they get a cut and color, but others just get a cut worth $50. If you have about half your clients spending $200 and half spending $50, your average customer is worth $125 per visit. And let's say each one visits about eight times per year. Each year, every customer you have is worth an average of $1000. If most stay with you for five years, each new customer you gain is worth about $5000.

- Lastly, take the example of a local bakery. You notice that most customers come in once a week and the average sale is $20. That customer is worth about $1000 per year to your business if they shop with you 50 weeks each year. Your customers tend to stick around for about three years, so any new customer you gain has the potential to be worth almost $3000.

If the bakery were to set a $6000 per-month advertising budget, how many customers would they need to acquire each month to break even with the advertising money they are spending? Well, their average customer value is $3000, so we divide that by the monthly budget of $6000 and find that they would need to attract about two new customers each month. If you end up getting six new customers a month with your $6000 investment, you're getting a 3:1 return on your advertising investment in gross revenue (before taking into account overhead, etc.), making it quite worth your while. You can take this number as a goal for your advertising.

ACCOUNTANTS VS. MARKETERS

The two feuding families in Shakespeare's Romeo and Juliet were the Montagues and the Capulets. Shakespeare never really explains why the families have been feuding for generations, but some speculate that it related to the prevalent theme of reason versus faith in the Renaissance period.

Though we don't know for sure why those families were mortal enemies, we can use them to illustrate the conflict that happens between marketers and accountants. Accountants like to see an expense directly reconciled with a return. Mass marketing doesn't work that way.

When you spend money on media advertising, the return does not always come immediately and you can't match exact sales with the advertising that drove those sales. While your advertising will almost always have a positive impact on your bottom line (if you have a salient and frequent message), it cannot be linked to exact results. So, it is an understandably uncomfortable place for an accountant to be. Because marketing is so difficult to measure, accountants don't like to see a big number next to your advertising budget.

Often, business owners will be scolded by their accountants for over-spending on advertising. The most successful business owners I've worked with always had aggressive (but responsible) advertising budgets, all while their accountants did not always agree with what they were spending. The results weren't black and white, but the stores always saw a healthy growth in sales year after year (or at least held their own during times when most businesses saw downturns).

Focusing on positive, big-picture results rather than trying to match exact advertising spends with exact customers is the kind of thinking that makes those businesses so successful. It has allowed them to not only survive, but to thrive in their competitive markets.

Spending on advertising, following the guidelines above, might be a terrifying endeavor for a small business—and especially for your accountant—but it is well worth the money in the end.

Of course, I'm not saying you should be irresponsible with your spending. My hope is that you will use the tools you've armed yourself with from this book to make wise advertising investments with a reasonable and consistent budget. Romeo and Juliet don't have to die at the end of your story.

HOMEWORK

1. Are there any aspects of your marketing that you need to change to fill in a missing layer of advertising? If so, what are the first things you will do?

2. What are you doing to keep in communication with your existing and past customers? What is one thing you can do to improve this?

3. Are you using discounts and sale events in a way that will build loyalty and enhance your regular branding?

4. What dollar amount did you spend on advertising each year for the past three years? What percentage of gross revenue did that equate to?

5. What is the average value of each of your customers?

   a. What is the average sale?

   b. How many times per year do they shop?

   c. How many years on average do they stay with your business?

6. Based on this chapter, should you be spending more or less than you have been on advertising?

CHAPTER 7

Measuring Success

"The customer's perception is your reality."

— Kate Zabriskie

At the end of the last chapter, we looked at the difference between how accountants look at money spent and how marketers see it. Marketers know that we can't match exact dollars spent with which customers come in to buy. However, understanding the overall impact your advertising makes on your bottom line is, in fact, hugely important and we'll get to that.

But first, let's look at one huge mistake businesses make when they advertise: not delivering on their promises.

DELIVERING ON YOUR PROMISES

In advertising, it is so nice to sit down and talk to media reps and copywriters and everyone involved in your campaigns about your ideal customer and what you can offer them. For a little while, you get to look at your business idealistically. You get to say who that perfect person will be who comes through the door, and imagine a perfect experience and a perfect transaction, and see how you will be the most helpful and positive business that person has ever come across. And then you get to imagine all the people they will tell about their amazing experience and all the happy customers you'll feature on your social media. It's great!

And I'm not here to tell you that it won't happen. Rather, I'm reminding you to make sure it *does* happen. When you're advertising, delivering on the promises you make in the messaging ensures that all the work you have done and all the money you have spent translates into revenue.

When you don't deliver on your promises, the effort you put into your advertising is a waste of time and money. If, once your advertising has done its job and gotten people to your door, you drop the ball, no one will stick around and make purchases. **Remember, the role of advertising is to get people to the door; it's your job to make the sale once they get there.**

Because we can do so much pre-shopping online, more and more customers are coming into stores ready to buy. They know what they want, how much it costs, and where else they can get it. If they are walking into your store, they likely plan to make a purchase that day. Too often, they end up changing their minds because of the experience they have once they get to the store or because the salesperson "un-sells" them.

So, before spending your money on advertising campaigns, make sure your customer experience is top-notch and that your staff and your merchandise convert your visitors into paying customers.

Your staff

Your staff are the people who represent you and your brand when customers come to see you. They are the first in-person interaction your customers will have with your company, so it's essential that they are prepared to do what you want them to do and that you support them through it.

Are you training them to walk the talk? Do you have a system your staff can follow so they can offer the same experience every time the customer visits? If your spa is promising customers a free foot massage with every pedicure, does that happen 100% of the time with every staff member?

Do you practice what you preach? The most successful small businesses I've worked with have an owner (or very special manager) who actively works in the store and models the behavior they want to see in their staff. There is no one better to show the best in customer service than the person who got into business to serve that customer and who is most affected by the bottom line.

Are you communicating regularly and effectively with your staff? It is so important that all staff members have the same information, and are kept in the loop about what the business is advertising.

There is a family of restaurants in our city that runs various promotions on the radio, from "kids eat free" to "half-price wine on Wednesdays," but the staff notoriously don't know what is going on. Customers have to ask about the promotion or don't bother asking and leave disappointed.

Staff should communicate the specials and promotions to the customer when they come in. Even if your advertising is doing its job, not everyone will be exposed to it. Plus, a lot of people may come in for the deal, but not want to appear cheap by asking about it. They will think, "Well, I thought it was a 20%-off deal on clothing today, but nobody's said anything and I don't see any signs saying that, so I must be wrong." And they may not want to return because you've created an uncomfortable situation for them.

You want to make it as easy as possible for your customers to do business with you and accept the offers that you're putting out there. Don't "test" the media by seeing who mentions your ad, because you're moreso testing your customers to see who is willing to bring it up, and I guarantee not everyone who heard or saw it will want to mention it.

It is good practice to post a copy of any print ad, radio script, online promotion, or TV script in the staff room. That way, if customers come in and request a specific product that they saw or ask for a special price that was in the ad, your staff can refer to their copy and confirm or clarify what the ad was offering. People don't always hear things correctly, so if they're saying that they heard you'll beat your competitor's price by $10, staff can double-check if that's really the promise you made.

Staff meetings are also important for ensuring your staff are all on the same page and they are familiar with the products you offer as well as the promotions you are running, so your customers have a consistent experience each time they show up.

Underestimating the level of communication that you need to have with your staff can happen to even the very best of businesses. I once took my kids to Brainsport as we were preparing for a trip to Europe and needed good walking shoes. I expected the usual help with choosing shoes and measuring feet, but none of that happened. The employee left us to our own devices and just waited for us to ask him for sizes. We were there for quite a while and kept trying to ask him what he would recommend, but he didn't offer much direction. We ended up leaving without making a purchase because we weren't able to find what we were looking for and couldn't risk making the wrong choice for such a big trip.

Because I was familiar with the usual experience I could expect at this store, I came back another day when I knew that other staff members would be working. Not many customers will do that. I shared this experience with the owner and of course he was troubled by what happened. He realized he'd started to take communication for granted and had assumed that the staff were being consistent with his promise based on their initial training. After our conversation, he renewed his focus on communication to ensure consistency in the service his store provides.

Your merchandise

When you advertise that you carry certain brands or that you're having a sale on a certain product, make sure that you have those products in stock. It sounds simple and maybe too obvious to you, but we all know how frustrating it is to hear about a promotion, visit the store, and leave with nothing because they don't have it in stock.

If you are sending out flyers with a multitude of products and half of those items are missing at the store, your customers will have a bad experience. If you run out, change the radio ad or cancel the social media post! Make sure the person in charge of your marketing is communicating with the person in charge of stock, so they both ensure that you can deliver on your promises.

YOUR CUSTOMER EXPERIENCE

Staff meetings, regular communication, and efficient systems are all key to ensuring that the customers have the same experience every time they visit you. Consistent delivery is just as important as consistency in your messaging. If you offer flavored coffee in the waiting room, offer it every single time. If you send out an agenda to a client before a meeting, do so every single time. There are many customer service resources and books to help you brush up on these things in more detail, but remember that following through on your promises every time is an important factor in successful marketing.

The promises you make to your customers about who you are, what you do, and what they can expect create the basis of your brand. But what ensures they will continue to do business with you and join your tribe is delivering on those promises. Whether it's your staff, your merchandise, or your customer experience, staying consistent with your message means your visitors will become and remain customers. And then, once you've resolved any issues on that front, you'll be more prepared to accurately measure the success of your advertising.

EVALUATING RESULTS

Ah, measurement in advertising. One of the biggest frustrations and most talked about issues in the advertising world. You're spending all this money, so how do you know that your efforts are not in vain?

I'd like to tell you that there is one simple, scientific method to figure out exactly how your media advertising dollars are performing and exactly who is coming in because of which advertising. But sadly, I cannot, and would question anyone who says they can. This is one of the key reasons so many advertisers are drawn to online advertising vehicles—traditional advertising is difficult to measure. But sticking to something because it is measurable isn't always the right thing, if it isn't as impactful (or it doesn't reach enough people). However, there are ways to determine whether your bigger picture advertising is working for you; it comes down to basic observation and common sense.

Before we get into that, let's talk once again about the difference between reaction and results. Many advertisers want to measure the reaction they get from their campaign. They want to know how many people liked them on Facebook and how many mention that they heard the ad. But what's most important when you're spending money on advertising are the *results* you are seeing. You need to know how many people are coming in the door or visiting your website and buying from you.

When I say the true results will show through observation, I mean that the only true test comes from feet through the door and dollars in your till. And the only real way to measure that is through watching what is happening in your store. Recognize the patterns of traffic and the familiar faces who are repeat customers. When you start a new advertising campaign, do you notice that you are seeing your past customers more often? Are you seeing new faces? You know what your sales have been month over month and year over year. Are they increasing at a faster rate than they were before? And are those increases due to a change in your product offering or maybe a competitor closing down, or do you have a feeling they are from your advertising?

One of the reasons the world is smitten with advertising online is because it is measurable. But people often get caught up in all of the things that can be measured and lose sight of the measurements that actually matter. Finding out how many likes and shares and impressions a post gets or how many clicks an ad receives can show you how far your advertising reaches and who has noticed the ad, but what matters more than all of that is how frequently people do what you asked them to do.

As an advertiser, you need to decide which actions you want people to take when they interact with you online, then measure your success in causing those actions to occur. Those are the only analytics that matter. For example, do you want people to spend time on your website? Sign up for your newsletter? Don't let yourself get lost in the popularity contest of *likes*; a like is a passive gesture and doesn't equate to results. Anything worth measuring should move the business needle and bring someone further down the sales funnel toward doing business with you.

STEPS TO MEASURE

Of course, you can easily find out how many likes or impressions you get with each online ad, and you can find out from your radio rep how many people are listening to the station, but to really see how your ads are impacting your sales, you need a way to measure the results. The best way to do *that* is by understanding where you are *before* launching your campaign, and then measuring what happens *during and after* that campaign.

Here is a sample measurement process:

1. **Get to know the status quo.** Before starting your advertising, observe your customers consistently. Make note of your repeat customers, the age and demographics of the people coming in, what they are coming in for, and how often they come in. Talk to your staff to get a better picture of this. Which days of the week are you busy? What are customers saying about why they stopped in? Note how things are right now.

2. **Know your numbers.** Take a look at your sales, year over year, for the past five years. Look at your highs and lows. Are they seasonal? Cyclical? Random? Again, get to know the status quo—how things are right now.

3. **Know your analytics.** You should have data on the traffic to your website and the people who are

searching for your business name or finding you through key search words on Google. Make sure you know the data on these things before your campaign.

4. **Launch only one new form of advertising at a time.** The only true way to see the impact your advertising efforts have is to observe the behavior of your customers and the difference in sales between when you weren't running a campaign and when you were. So, if you launch a "media mix," or many things at once, it will be impossible to truly know which activities have the biggest impact. If you're launching a radio campaign, that should be the only thing you add for the first six months or more. Remember, it will take time for you to build visibility and credibility with your audience before the advertising will start to pay off.

5. **Don't try to do self-guided "how did you hear about us" surveys.** It's common for business owners to have their staff poll their customers with that question, or ask them to fill out a survey and check off how they heard about you. But think about your response when you're asked this kind of question for another business. You think, "Well, I heard about it on the TV news I think, but I also drive past it all the time, and my friend reminded me that I can get what I need here. So, I guess I'll say word of mouth." Usually, people will answer with just the most recent way they were reminded about your store, but not credit all the other ways that have made them aware of you over the years. Often, they heard about you and then Googled you for more information, and so they'll say they found you on Google.

6. **Watch trends.** Keep watching your customers (okay, that sounds like I'm telling you to be a stalker)—but I mean watch the patterns, the changes in traffic, the new faces, perhaps the younger (or older) people starting to come in. Watch your numbers. Are the highs and lows in sales becoming less extreme? Are you trending upward more quickly than you had been historically? If you're advertising to a younger crowd than you traditionally had as customers, are you starting to see younger people come in more consistently? Are people requesting things you've been highlighting in your ads?

7. **Revisit your analytics.** Since you know what your web traffic was before you started to advertise, now make a note of what has changed. Increased traffic to your website can be an early indicator that your audience is taking notice, even before they start buying. If you launch an ad campaign and your web traffic goes up substantially, you can see that you are successfully building interest in what you have going on.

    One time, I helped a property developer advertise a new set of acreage lots he had just put on the market. His web traffic skyrocketed the day we launched the media campaign and stayed high throughout the campaign. In fact, knowing the status quo beforehand helped him diagnose a fundamental problem with his product. Web traffic skyrocketed, but the customers coming to his site were spending time there, then clicking through to a different set of acreage properties he had listed and calling him with interest in buying those instead. It showed him that the advertising was, in fact, working to pique interest, but the properties he was advertising were not desirable to the market. People were shopping them and choosing not to buy.

If he hadn't known his traffic numbers beforehand, he would have just blamed the advertising, saying it didn't work. But with more information, he could see that the advertising was getting people to the door, but he wasn't able to convert interested buyers on those particular properties.

If nothing is changing after you've given a reasonable amount of time to an ad campaign, that's when you question your strategy.

Now, if you want to do more than one thing at a time right off the bat—for example, a combination of billboards and newspaper and social media—of course that is fine if you have the budget to do each thing well. But you just have to be okay with seeing a change and not knowing exactly where the customers are coming from or assume they are being influenced by a combination of your efforts.

SAMPLE SURVEY[1]

If you are concerned with the effectiveness of your ad campaign, you can employ the services of a market research firm to assess ad recall and effectiveness. This doesn't need to be an overly expensive and involved process. Essentially, when they measure ad recall and effectiveness for you, it will boil down to the following key concepts:

- **Claimed recall:** Do people recall seeing/hearing your ads on an unaided basis (without being shown the ad during the survey).

- **Proven recall:** Of those who say they saw your ads, did they describe the ad in sufficient detail to prove that they really did recall the ad? For an insurance broker/agency, this is the difference between responses such as, "It was about insurance," and, "They talked about being open later than anyone else and open on Sunday, too."

- **Prompted recall:** Do they remember the ad if they are shown it again?

- **Brand link:** Can they name the company or brand the ad was for? You may think, "Why ask that…you just showed them the ad!" Amazingly, brand link isn't universal, even after just seeing the ad, but it is an essential metric in measuring ad effectiveness. For example, if only 40% of the people who saw your ad knew it was for you, then 60% of your ad spend is wasted. Maybe they didn't notice the ad (didn't break through the clutter) or the ad didn't connect to your specific brand and you just promoted your competitors (poor brand link).

- **Message comprehension:** After seeing the ad, can they tell you what it was about? What was it trying to say? If people don't interpret your ad the way you want them to, it isn't working. These open-ended comments can be broken down into "correct" and "incorrect" mentions. Again, if only 20% of people who saw your ad knew it was for you *and* understood the intended message, 80% of your money is wasted.

- **Ad resonance:** How effective was the ad? Finally, just because someone saw the ad, knew it was for you and understood the message, does not mean they connected with it. Could they relate to it? Did they find it informative? Are they tuning it out because they don't need what it's selling or because it's gotten stale?

As mentioned earlier, research on ad effectiveness doesn't need to be expensive. Many research companies offer a product called an omnibus. Essentially, clients pay a per-question fee to add questions to a survey that runs occasionally—usually monthly. Your questions appear on the survey along with those from their other clients. Together, you all cover the costs for the research company to run the survey. You don't see the answers to other client questions, nor do they see yours. This is the least expensive option if you want to engage a research firm.

Even if you don't have the budget to hire a firm, you can carry out research on advertising effectiveness yourself with your customer email list, if you wish. Below are a standard set of questions you can use either in an omnibus or on your own through an email list of your customers (note that the first two questions will result in slightly skewed responses if you are sending the survey out to your email list since they know you are the one conducting the research):

1. Have you seen or heard advertising for the following service providers lately? (Claimed recall.)

   [include a list of you and your competitors to keep respondents guessing who the survey is for]

2. Please describe the advertising you saw/heard for [insert your company name]. What did it say? What did it show? What was it about? (Proven recall.)

3. Have you seen the following advertisement(s) lately? (Prompted recall.)

   [insert ad(s)]

   Yes/No

Generally, ask the following questions for video ads only—TV ads, pre-roll, etc.

4. What company was this ad for?

5. What was the ad telling you? In your opinion, what was the main message?

6. Please rate your level of agreement with each of the following statements regarding the ad. [Strongly agree/Somewhat agree/Disagree]

   - The ad told you something that had meaning to you
   - The ad was very enjoyable
   - You are getting tired of seeing the ad
   - The ad increased your interest in the brand
   - The ad presents the company in a different way from competitors

It is best to conduct this research during or right after the campaign. That will be the point at which recall is at its highest.

One of my clients recently had a very good experience when she hired a research company to study the effectiveness of her media advertising. For a reasonable price, they conducted a focus group. That was very helpful to this particular client as she received tons of insights about what people knew about her business and why they shopped her (or didn't). It reaffirmed that her advertising was making an impact, because when people were asked open-ended questions, they used the unique wording to describe the business she had been using in her commercials.

• • •

When it comes to measuring the effectiveness of advertising, it is more of a general observation than a specific cause-and-effect. However, there are some ways to ensure your measurement efforts are effective:

- Deliver on the promises you make in your advertising—you want to know that when your customers walk in the door, they aren't disappointed with their experience or "un-sold" by your staff.

- Measure each method of advertising by adding only one type of media at a time and observing the changes in your customer base and their activity—you can see if their behavior changes, if their demographics change, and if you are seeing more new customers. When you compare these observations and data to the baseline, you can see the impact your campaign is having.

- Hire a research company to run a survey about your ads and your customers' recall if you want to measure in more detail. If you don't want to or can't afford a third-party, you can do the survey yourself through your mailing list.

Overall, the point in all of this is to figure out where your advertising dollars are being wasted so you can optimize your future campaigns. If you see that one specific channel or schedule doesn't work, you can try another. If one works well, you can continue using it and growing with it. If nothing seems to work, it could be your messaging itself or customer experience that needs work.

Advertising is a learning process, so not everything will work every time. As your business matures and your advertising grows, you can spend more time and money optimizing your ads, figuring out how to make improvements, and creating a playbook for your advertising efforts. To help you get started off on the right foot, I've created an Action Plan guide, which you'll find at the end of this book. Before you get to that, answer these questions about your business:

HOMEWORK

1. Are you clearly and consistently communicating to your staff what is expected of them?

2. Does the experience your customers have in-store reflect the promises you are making in your ads?

3. What three things can you do to improve your delivery when a customer walks in the door?

4. What actions do you want people to take when they interact with you online? Is your online presence and messaging set up to lead visitors to take those actions?

5. If surveyed, what two things do you hope your customers would recall about your business from your advertising?

6. Summarize the status quo in your business in the following areas:

    a. Current customer profiles and traffic patterns.

    b. Sales, year over year, for the past five years and seasonal trends.

    c. Current website traffic, time spent on your site, and resulting activity.

7. What results would you like to see over the next year from your advertising?

Chapter 8

Wrapping Up

"Many a small thing has been made large by the right kind of advertising."

—Mark Twain

There are endless ways to view advertising, and thousands of books written on the subject. If the content you've read in this book feels right and rings true for you, I hope you take it and run with it—and enjoy immense business success from your efforts.

To help you on this path, there is still one last thing to do: develop your action plan. You can find an Action Plan guide in the next section of this book.

Key takeaways

Although there is a lot of content within these pages, there are a few important themes that consistently come up. They are the basis of my business coaching and the platform from which you can build your advertising. You can continue to use this book as a reference while your business grows and changes, but here are the ideas I hope you take with you right now:

- Your brand is the story people tell about you when you're not in the room. You have a wonderful story—shout it from the rooftops! Let people know why you're here and why they should love you. And it all starts with the customer and the message; people don't want to hear what you do, they want to hear why you do it and why they should care. That's what makes your message salient. WIIFM should be your favorite radio station!

- Stop chasing the unpredictable, perfect moment to reach your customer. Convince them of your worth before they need you and then sit back, relax, and let your well-planned advertising do its job. As you're making each advertising decision, measure it against CCF (consistency, creativity, and frequency) and figure out where it fits into the message you want to send (or if it fits at all). Not all advertising is created equal nor should it be expected to bring you the same results.

- Cast the biggest net you can, with CCF, with the budget you have and you will catch more fish. Figure out how to best marry your online activities with your intrusive advertising through mass media and you will become a force to be reckoned with.

- Advertising, no matter how amazing it is, can only get people to the door. Make sure that you are "wowing" them every time they visit so they buy from you and tell their friends to buy from you, too.

Overall, do as much as you can to be *sought after* by your customers by using intrusive, active channels and put less focus on waiting in passive places to be *found*. The more successful you are at this, the greater the chance you will be *picked*.

You don't have to go it alone

My own experience has taught me that it is hard to clearly see what you should do for your own business advertising because you are too close to it—it's hard to read the label from inside the bottle. If you feel that you need an outside, unemotional perspective to help you see your company the way it really is and to uncover your blind spots, that's the role a business advisor can play.

An advisor can look at your business the way the customer would see it, but with a more educated view on business principles. They can see what you are doing and if it is working from an objective point of view to make sure your story is clear and that you're not answering questions in your messaging that nobody is asking. Without the emotional attachment you have to your business, a coach can help get you on the right course and keep you accountable to staying there, while supporting you when it comes to making decisions that are best for your business.

At Boost Strategic Coaching, we work through the concepts in this book as part of our clients' business development activities. Under our model, your coach becomes your "co-pilot" and you work together to set goals, develop plans, and weed through options. We don't look at just your advertising; we work with you to network, develop your direct sales, and build your overall marketing strategies to further your business development while avoiding costly mistakes. If you feel you would like a Boost Coach to support you in implementing this material, please feel free to email us at info@boostcoaching.ca or check out our website at www.boostcoaching.ca

GO FORTH AND PROSPER

In the following pages, we'll go through the steps to creating your advertising Action Plan. Completing the action plan will take you into more depth and leave you with a playbook ready to implement. Everything that you need to move ahead is in this book. It doesn't have to be used in its entirety, but it does have to be used. Put it to work and see your bottom line grow.

YOUR ACTION PLAN

Let's get to work. This is where you commit answers to the questions we've been asking throughout this book and dive a little deeper. If you've been keeping up with answering the homework questions as you finished each chapter, this exercise will go fairly quickly. If not, take your time with it.

Don't attempt to complete this all in one sitting— that would be no fun. Instead, I recommend setting aside an hour or two each week for the next few weeks when you can find a quiet place, sit down with a cup of coffee, and start developing your plan.

As you go through, think about the ideal marketing plan you would envision, but also consider the reality of your business, budget, and time constraints. **You'll find page references in square brackets [ ] next to some of the questions so you can refer back and refresh your memory on the topics.**

You can find a downloadable workbook for answering these questions at www.boostcoaching/hands-on

STEP 1 – UNDERSTAND THE STATUS QUO

It's impossible to know where to go with your advertising unless you first have a clear picture of where you are right now. We'll start out by defining who you are, who your audience is, and what the market is saying right now and reviewing what you're already doing with your marketing. Then, you'll have a basis on which to set some goals and move forward.

1. WHO ARE YOU?

Before we know what to say, we have to know who we are. Since you will want to make sure your message is consistent with your business and the services and products you offer, start by figuring out what type of business you are in, the reasons people buy from you, and what you do better than your competition. Answer these questions:

WHAT IS YOUR BUSINESS?

1. Do you sell a "need" or a "want"? [30]

2. Do you sell a product or service? [30]

3. Why did you choose this business? [33]

4. What do you love about the work you do?

WHY DO PEOPLE BUY FROM YOU?

1. What are the practical reasons that someone would be motivated to buy from you? [34]

2. What are the emotional reasons?

WHAT DO YOU DO BETTER THAN YOUR COMPETITION?

1. What does your company do better than anyone else? Do you sell better products? Offer better service? Is your store unique or memorable? Is your staff better? Where is the biggest opportunity for you? [39]

2. How do these benefits compare to those of your three main competitors?

2. WHO IS YOUR AUDIENCE?

Now that you know who you are as a business, let's look at who you currently serve. Too often, messaging gets lost on the audience because it's written in words only the business owner understands. They often over-complicate the message and as soon as you make your customer work too hard to understand you, you've lost them and they'll go somewhere else. It's important to speak to the customer in their language, so you first need to get to know the customer. Answer these questions:

WHO ARE THEY?

1. Who do you currently serve? [31]

2. What are the demographics of your typical customer? [57]

3. What do they do and like? What kinds of people are they?

WHERE ARE THEY?

1. On which social media platform(s) do your customers hang out?

2. Where are they looking for information or having conversations about your industry? (ie. if you're an interior decorator, your customers may go to Pinterest for design inspiration.)

3. Where do groups of your customers congregate? (Professional associations, events, specific workplaces, etc.)

WHAT LANGUAGE DO THEY SPEAK?

1. What is important to your customers? [65]

2. What are three pains your customers complain about?

3. What words do they use to describe their lifestyle? Their problems? Their preferences?

Field work: this may be a good time to talk directly to your customers. Ask them the above questions and find out what they look for in your business category and what motivates them to buy. Go on a fact-finding mission and buy a few customers a cup of coffee to chat.

3. YOUR CUSTOMER EXPERIENCE

As you know, it is your customer experience that will make or break whether your marketing efforts turn into sales. Advertising gets people to the door; it's your job to make the sale once they get there. Before advertising, make sure to study your customer experience and staff performance. To figure out where you can make improvements, answer these questions:

1. Are you clearly and consistently communicating to your staff what is expected of them? [249]

2. Are you sharing your advertising messages with your staff to ensure they can deliver on your promises? [249]

3. Does the experience your customers have in store reflect the promises you are making in your ads? [252]

4. What three things can you do to improve your delivery when a customer walks in the door? [252]

YOUR CUSTOMER JOURNEY MAP [66]

Create a journey map of a typical customer who visits your business. Consider every step they take to get into your store, what they do when they get there, and everything they do with their purchase once they leave. Once you have created your journey map, answer the following questions:

1. Can you identify any common pain points in the process your customers go through?

2. What are some simple steps you can take to improve their experience?

3. Is there anything about the journey that is extra special that you should be mentioning in your advertising?

4. YOUR CURRENT MESSAGING

When it comes to messaging, it's important to find out the story already being told about you and see if it matches what you want the story to be. Answer these questions:

HOW DOES THE MARKET SEE YOU?

1. What are people currently saying about you? [45]

2. What feeling is associated with your business?

3. Are there any misperceptions in the market about you? What are they?

4. What do you wish people knew about you that they don't?

Field work: if you're having trouble answering the above questions because you don't know how the market sees you, this would be a good time to do some market research. Think of what information would be helpful for you to gather from your customers to get a clear picture of where you are now. Again, buy some people a coffee and pick their brains about the questions you have, employ the methods outlined in Chapter 2 [44] to create your own survey, or hire a research firm to conduct a study on your behalf.

WHAT ARE YOU DOING TO CONTROL THE STORY?

1. What were the last three messages you put into the market?

    a. Do those messages all contribute to the same idea or introduce different ideas?

    b. Do they make clear the *benefit* to your customers or just the details about your business? (Think WIIFM!) [70]

2. Does your message fit with the story you want to be telling?

3. Do your messages clearly state to the audience why you exist?

4. What have you done today, this week, and this month to share this information with the market?

5. Do your commercials aim to persuade, inform, or simply entertain your audience?

5. Current marketing

Now take a look at what you are already doing with your advertising, how it's going so far, and if you are seeing the results you want. This will help you find gaps and opportunities for improvement later on in the planning process. Answer these questions:

1. Which layers of advertising have you achieved with your marketing? [131]

2. Have you attained CCF? [117]

    a. Where are you achieving consistency (C)? [118]

    b. Are you sending out your creative message in a compelling way (C)? [119]

    c. On which media are you running your message with frequency (F)? [119]

3. How much of your effort is put into being *sought*? How much of it is in waiting to be *found*? [190]

6. Your baseline

Summarize the status quo in your business in the following areas:

1. Current customer profiles and traffic patterns.

2. Sales, year over year, for the past five years and seasonal trends.

3. Average weekly new customer traffic to your store.

4. Current website traffic, time spent on your site, and resulting activity.

5. Your social media engagement.

Step 2 – Set Goals

Now that you have a clear picture of the "status quo," it's time to examine what changes you'd like to make to *what is* and set goals for *what you want it to be*. When looking at the following questions, go back and read your answers from the last section. This can help you spot gaps and find opportunities moving forward.

1. Who do you want to be?

Knowing who you are and who you want to be will help you figure out the steps you need to take. Consider your ideal business when you answer these questions:

1. Is there anything about your business, product, or service offering that you would like to change or improve?

2. Is there anything you should get rid of in order to simplify or streamline your offering to the market?

2. Who do you want to serve?

It's impossible to create effective messaging until you first determine exactly who it is you're targeting with it. Think of your ideal customers and compare them to the customers you currently have. It's helpful to imagine one specific person when you are working through this section. Then answer these questions:

1. Who do you *want* to serve? Are they the same as your current customers or do you want to reach a new audience? [31]

2. What does your target market need from you? What *benefits* do you offer them? What problem(s) do you solve for them? [34, 39]

3. Is there anything in your business that currently doesn't support this?

3. DEVELOPING YOUR MESSAGE

Now that you know who you want to serve and what you want to serve them with, you can start to figure out what to say to them. First consider the following:

1. What feeling do you want associated with your business? [15]

2. What would you like the story to be? [15]

Next, thinking about the benefits you want to offer to your customer, answer the following questions [53]:

1. What do I do?

2. Why does it matter?

3. Who should care?

Consider what your advertising has been saying as compared to what you should be saying to reach your ideal customers. What should you add or change to the messaging you've already been sending out? Answer these questions:

1. What about your message could or should change to reach the people you want to talk to?

2. How do you want your ads to feel?

3. Which elements (jingles, endorsements, etc.) do you think would fit within your story? (Note: This may be something to make a point of asking your advertising consultants about in the next phase of planning.) [82]

4. SETTING YOUR BUDGET

Your exposure budget should be about 4–12% of your gross revenue, but more if you are just starting out. Take a look at what you are currently spending, factors like your level of competition, your location, and average value of a customer, and adjust your marketing budget accordingly.

1. What dollar amount did you spend on advertising each year for the past three years? What percentage of gross revenue did that equate to?

2. What is the average value of your customer? To determine this, answer the following questions [241]:

    a. What is the average sale?

    b.   How many times per year does the typical customer shop with you?

    c.   How many years on average do they stay with your business?

3.   What should your marketing budget be? How many new customers do you need per month to break even on your advertising? [236, 241]

4.   Should you be spending more or less than you have been on advertising?

5. Desired outcomes

Before starting a campaign, you first need to figure out where you are, and then you'll want to determine where you intend to go. What are your advertising goals and what do you expect to see once your campaign begins? Now is a good time to determine which data points you want to examine throughout your campaign.

Note: When I say "data points," that does not necessarily mean statistics. You can observe trends and patterns, or you can collect data from surveys. There are benefits to both. What is important is that you are observing and understanding your customers' behavior.

1.   What results would you like to see over the next year from your advertising? What are your advertising goals (more web traffic, more sales,

new customers, happier customers, maintain market share, etc.)?

2. Which five pieces of data will help you determine if you've achieved these results? [255]

3. Will you work with a third-party to track your results? If so, which one and how much will that cost? [258]

Step 3 – Consider your options

1. The Advertising Toolbox

Now that you know who you are targeting and how much you will spend, it's time to figure out which advertising vehicles will be a good fit to reach your audience and keep within your budget.

Recall the Advertising Toolbox layers and their purposes:

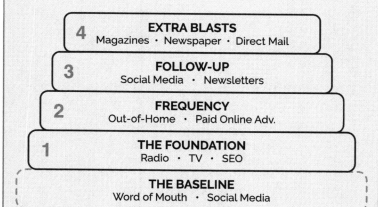

4 — EXTRA BLASTS
Magazines · Newspaper · Direct Mail

3 — FOLLOW-UP
Social Media · Newsletters

2 — FREQUENCY
Out-of-Home · Paid Online Adv.

1 — THE FOUNDATION
Radio · TV · SEO

THE BASELINE
Word of Mouth · Social Media

WHERE YOU EXIST
Store · Website

Answer the following:

1. Which layers do you have covered with your current advertising? [131]

2. Are you currently missing any layers that you need to fill in? If so, which one(s)? [131]

3. What is one thing you can do to improve how you keep in communication with your existing customers? [172]

4. What actions do you want people to take when they interact with you online? Do you need to make any changes to your online messaging to make that happen?

5. Are you using discounts and sale events in a way that will build loyalty and enhance your regular branding? [231]

2. COLLECT INFORMATION ON YOUR OPTIONS

Make a note of the layer(s) you feel you need to add, remove, or improve on and consider the following:

SELF-MANAGED OPTIONS

If you would like to manage some of the advertising yourself, research options for social media management platforms and newsletter automation so you can pre-plan and automate these activities. For the things you'll need help with, consider the following:

WHO DO YOU ALREADY WORK WITH?

List the media you already employ. If you work with media reps or marketing agencies, list who you work with and which media they cover. Set up a time to meet with them to make sure they are clear on your needs and goals. Tweak and make changes where necessary to make sure your activities are all aligned with your objectives.

WHICH MEDIA DO YOU WANT TO ADD? [129]

If you already run advertising, or if you are just starting out, list the types of advertising vehicles you want to work with to match the Advertising Toolbox layers you would like to fulfill. Keep this section broad by listing only the categories (TV, radio, etc.).

WHO SHOULD YOU WORK WITH?

Now that you know which categories you want to explore, make a list of the media outlets and online marketing firms you might want to work with. Find their contact information and set up meetings or consultations with their advertising reps. This can be a time-consuming process and you won't want to change or add many things at once (or it will be difficult to measure and track results), so don't feel like you need to meet with every company in town before doing anything.

If you want to focus on online marketing first, meet with two or three firms in that category to compare recommendations and pricing. If you have one or two types of mass media on your immediate wish list, meet with a representative from each of those to get an idea of what those media can offer and what they would charge. In these meetings, find out the following:

- Their audience (keep in mind the more "mass" the media, the less targeted it will be, and that's ok).

- The schedule or plan they would recommend to meet your objectives (year-round CCF, periodic blasts, extra frequency, etc.).

- The creative direction they would recommend to tell your story.

- How much it will cost for both the schedule and the creative services. With some media like radio and print, the writing, design, and production would be no extra charge; however, with out-of-home advertising and television there would be a cost associated with production.

- If they offer discounts for longer-term commitments (like 6 months or a year).

- The opportunities available for partnership in "extras" like contests, community involvement, morning show features, etc.

Note: Not every representative who sells advertising products will focus on CCF. In fact, many will be surprised if you ask them for a quote for year-round advertising, so know what your objectives are before you go in and determine whether the person you meet with can fulfill your requests and add value to the planning.

STEP 4 – TAKE ACTION

Now that you have figured out your market and your message, and you've collected pricing and information from media and online representatives, you can put your plan in place. Here are the steps to take to get your marketing up and firing on all cylinders:

1. LOCATION AND STAFF

- If you uncovered anything that needs updating to your storefront or signage to be more noticeable and attractive to your walk or drive-by traffic, make those changes. [213]

- If your website needs upgrading and a stronger call to action, facilitate those changes. [214]

- Schedule regular staff meetings or educational opportunities for your staff and start posting your ads for them to see. [249]

2. WORD-OF-MOUTH AND SOCIAL MEDIA

If you have chosen to manage some of the marketing yourself when it comes to things like social media and newsletters, set up a system to make this easier and automated for you if you have not yet done so. Then decide how far in advance you'd like to schedule your activity (monthly? quarterly?) and set aside time in your calendar at regular intervals to update content. [172]

3. Advertising Toolbox Layers 1 to 4

Decide what you're going to keep of your current advertising, what you're going to get rid of, and what you're going to add. (Keep in mind that you don't want to add too many things at once because it will be difficult to measure the results.) Then decide on the timing for your changes and schedule meetings with the representatives involved. [131]

4. Your storybook

To ensure that you don't lose focus throughout the year and that you build a consistent story in the market, use the tools we talked about in Chapter 4: the creative manual and the creative calendar. The creative manual (your book cover) is a list of the elements that will be part of your advertising all year and a variation of this list will be consistent across all media. The creative calendar (the chapters of your book) is the schedule you follow to ensure that by the end of the year you have told all of the chapters of your story).

Develop your creative manual [106]:

1.   List the elements that will be consistent in all of your advertising (business name, tagline, location, etc.).

2.   Create a version of this for each of the media you are using. (Your radio creative manual would include different elements than your magazine one.)

Develop your creative calendar [108]:

1. Sit down with a calendar and plot out what you need to be talking about in each season, around special occasions, end of season sales, annual events, etc. Also make a list of all the things you want to get across during the year, and devote time for focusing on each point sometime in the year. (Remember: one thought, one spot.)

2. Schedule social media ads and posts based on your creative calendar.

3. Share your creative calendar with the creative teams from the media outlets you've chosen to advertise with.

5. ENSURE CONSISTENCY

Making a plan and sticking to it is often where marketers struggle because they either want to give up too early or they want to change their message too soon.

1. How can you ensure your messaging stays consistent throughout the year?

2. What are two things you can do to remind yourself that advertising is a long game?

Now that everything is set up, you can get back to running your business and start watching for the results you've worked so hard to create.

STEP 5 – MEASURE AND MANAGE

Good advertising is a marathon, not a sprint. The easiest way to determine what is working and what is not is to only add one new element at a time. This is the only way for you to attribute your results to the specific medium. If you don't want to add only one at a time, that's fine, as long as you are okay with not knowing *exactly* what is causing the change—but you should still measure the results you get.

1. MEASURE AGAINST YOUR BASELINE

In Step 1, you summarized the status quo in your business. Now, keep track and see where changes are happening to:

1. Current customer profiles and traffic patterns.

2. Sales month over month and year over year, and if seasonal ups and downs smooth out.

3. Average weekly new customer traffic to your store.

4. Changing website traffic, time spent on your site, and resulting activity.

5. Your social media engagement.

2. MEASURE AGAINST DESIRED OUTCOMES

For each of the existing and new activities you are implementing, go back to Step 2.5. Look at the outcomes you wanted to see and compare them to what is happening now.

1. What changes do you see based on your advertising goals (more web traffic, more sales, new customers, happier customers, etc.)?

2. Look at the pieces of data you listed in Question 2 of your desired outcomes. How have the numbers changed?

3. If you are seeing positive changes, what do you believe is the top contributor to those results?

4. If you aren't seeing the changes you expected, what could be the problem? How can you figure this out?

5. What should you adjust to start seeing better results?

After your advertising has been running for a reasonable length of time (6 months or more), you can decide if and when you want to employ a market research firm to measure awareness in the market based on your campaign.

STEP 6 – RINSE AND REPEAT

When you think of advertising as an ongoing part of your business, there is no start or end. As business owners, we strive to be able to "set it and forget it" by putting management systems in place and booking long-term campaigns then giving them time to do their job. But while you have your head down running your business, it's important to keep track of your advertising in your peripheral vision and nudge and adjust it as your business, products, industry, market, and customers change.

At least once a year, set aside time to take a look at your status quo, set new goals as you achieve old ones, reevaluate your budget, take a look at your options, and adjust where necessary. Basically, fill out the Action Plan workbook every year—you'll probably be surprised to see how much has changed each time you do it.

You are armed with all the tools you need to succeed in advertising and have worked *very* hard. You've made it all the way to the end of this section, now go forth and enjoy the fruits of your labor!

Acknowledgments

Working on this immense project has reminded me of how many people in my life are there to cheer me on, support me, and be excited for the path I find myself following. Throughout many months my set response of, "I can't, I'm editing," when invited to visit or socialize was always met by words of encouragement from dear friends and family alike.

First, I would like to thank Christopher Flett whose initial comment of, "You need to write a book on this stuff," was met by my disbelieving nervous laughter. I am so thankful that he heard what I had to say on the subject of advertising and thought enough of it to bring up the idea again and then inspire and guide me into getting my ideas onto paper so they might be usable to business owners beyond those I can reach in person.

I am grateful for the brilliant work of my editor, Gillian Katsoulis of GillianRyan Publishing, who worked tirelessly to help me turn my ideas and tangents and unfinished thoughts into something that looks like a grownup wrote it. The attention and input she contributed made it clear that she cared for the project as if it were her own.

Thank you to Rawlco Radio, and most especially Cliff Lesko, for allowing me the opportunity to start and grow my career in the fun and dynamic world of radio. My time there was enriched by unique opportunities to learn, surrounded by people and a company culture that truly care about and are driven by the success of their clients.

A huge thank you to my collaborators and contributors, in particular my good friend Lang McGilp of Insightrix Research who wrote the market research material in the book and Craig Silliphant of Rawlco Radio for his creative writing contributions.

I would like to thank the various subjects of this book for their time and willingness to be printed for all to see; Kevin Robinson (Eb's Source for Adventure), Brian Michasiw (Brainsport), Alex Istifo (Sardinia Family Restaurant), Joe & Jennifer Giocoli (Precision Auto Body), Bob Gibb and Laverne Vigoren (the Awl Shoppe). Working with exceptional business owners like you over the years has been a privilege. As well, Aim Electric, Daisy's Restaurant, JobShop and the rest of the businesses in my community who have made an impression on me with their brilliant advertising. Thank you also to the friends and colleagues who helped improve the manuscript, including Cam Bedry, Laurie Friesen, Jennifer Giocoli, Kristy Jackson, Carla Browne, Greg Malin, Stuart Sutton, Tatrina Tai, and Lang McGilp.

Also thank you to the following great people who leant their expertise and experiences to the book content: Amanda Soulodre (Saskatoon HOME Magazine), Mechell Smith (NationAd), Katie Bosler (Comcast Spotlight), Adrienne Sellers (Entercom Seattle), Laurel Douglas and Danielle Hoffer (Women's Enterprise Centre of BC), Stacey Cattell (Regina Pats & Rawlco Radio), Robina Palmer (Sun City Physiotherapy, Kelowna BC), Jennifer Shewchuk

(Global TV Saskatoon), Tyler Babiy (T Squared Social), Cary Bowman (LB Distillers), Don Ramage (Focal Point Business Coaching & Training), Clay Sparks (Breathe Cycle Studio), Shanna Lux, and Christine Thille (Rawlco Radio). As well, Greg Harrison and Craig Silliphant of Rawlco Radio for teaching me so much about outstanding creative writing, and Angelo Frassetto and Kyle Kildaw for the great fun we had in creating the Rocco ads for Precision Auto Body over the years.

David Molesky and Heather Adams, my design team from Rock & Bloom, are brilliant and continue to blow me away with their contribution to my projects, including the cover design and graphics for this book. They get me.

Last, but certainly not least, I am eternally grateful for my husband Greg and our three children, Elliott, Allister, and Julia. It is impossible to put into words the place these four souls hold in my heart. Thank you for your patience, understanding, and encouragement throughout the challenging journey of writing this book and through all of the crazy endeavors you've seen me through. None of them could have happened without a safe place to land.

NOTES

CHAPTER 1

1. For a condensed summary of the book, check out Sinek's Ted Talk on the subject.

2. I am a graduate of the Wizard Academy and have spent many years studying Mr. Williams' teachings and putting them into practice with my clients.

3. Roy H. Williams, "The Future of Advertising," *The Monday Morning Memo*, May 24, 2004, http://www.mondaymorningmemo.com/newsletters/the-future-of-advertising

4. Howard Schultz, *Pour Your Heart into It: How Starbucks Built a Company One Cup at a Time*, New York: Hyperion, 1997, pg. 255

CHAPTER 2

1. Thank you to Cary Bowman of LB Distillers, Candace Ippolito of Sask Made Marketplace, Don Ramage of Focal Point Business Coaching & Training, Carla Browne of Real Property Management Professionals, and Clay Sparks of Breathe Cycle Studio for sharing with me their inspiration for starting their businesses.

2. Market research material in this chapter contributed by Lang McGilp of Insightrix Research.

CHAPTER 3

1. Market research material in this chapter contributed by Lang McGilp of Insightrix Research.

CHAPTER 4

1. Radio script contributed by Craig Silliphant, Creative Director at Rawlco Radio Saskatoon.

2. Radio script contributed by Craig Silliphant, Creative Director at Rawlco Radio Saskatoon.

3. Radio script contributed by Craig Silliphant, Creative Director at Rawlco Radio Saskatoon.

4. Magazine creative manual contributed by Amanda Soulodre, owner of Saskatoon HOME magazine.

5. Steve Topper, "Are You Advertising to a Moving Parade or a Standing Army?," *Deluxe*, August 31, 2010, http://fi.deluxe.com/community-blog/financial-marketing-insights/are-you-advertising-to-a-moving-parade-or-a-standing-army

CHAPTER 5

1. Williams refers to sleep as the ever-faithful street sweeper; cleansing our minds and helping us cope with the sounds, sights, problems, emotions, and distractions of our day in Roy H. Williams, *Secret Formulas of the Wizard of Ads* (Austin, TX: Bard Press, 1999), 98-99.

2. Williams explains newspaper as a sprinter; an information-delivery vehicle that reaches only those buyers who are in the market right now for the product, but fails to reach those who are not consciously in the market for the advertised product or service in Roy H. Williams, *Secret Formulas of the Wizard of Ads* (Austin, TX: Bard Press, 1999), 96-97

3. "The Global Standard for Measuring Radio Advertising Effectiveness," *Canadian Broadcast Sales*, accessed April 24, 2017, http://www.radiocbs.com/showpage.php?pageid=19

4. "Radio: The Online Multiplier," *Radiocentre*, accessed April 23, 2017, http://www.radiocentre.org/studies/radio-the-online-multiplier/

5. "The Nielsen Total Audience Report: Q1 2016," *Neilsen*, June 27, 2016, http://www.nielsen.com/us/en/insights/reports/2016/the-total-audience-report-q1-2016.html, as cited in "AM/FM Reach is High; Time-Spent Is Nuanced," *RAIN News*, June 27, 2016, http://rainnews.com/amfm-reach-is-high-time-spent-is-nuanced-nielsen-report

6. "Audio Today: Radio 2016 – Appealing Far and Wide," *Nielsen*, February 25, 2016, http://www.nielsen.com/us/en/insights/reports/2016/audio-today-radio-2016-appealing-far-and-wide.html and "State of the News Media 2015," *Pew Research Center*, April 2015, http://www.journalism.org/files/2015/04/final-state-of-the-news-media1.pdf, as cited in "Radio Facts and Figures," *News Generation*, accessed on March 18, 2017, http://www.newsgeneration.com/broadcast-resources/radio-facts-and-figures

7. Eric Sass, "Half of U.S. Listeners Tune into Online Radio," *Media Daily News*, March 5, 2014, http://www.mediapost.com/publications/article/220860/half-of-us-listeners-tune-into-online-radio.html

8. Based on US listening data from Peter Nowak, "The Skeptics Said Streaming Music Would Kill Satellite Radio. They Were Wrong," *Canadian Business*, April 7, 2016, http://www.canadianbusiness.com/innovation/the-skeptics-said-streaming-music-would-kill-satellite-radio-they-were-wrong and US population data from "U.S. Population," *WorldoMeters*, accessed March 12, 2017, http://www.worldometers.info/world-population/us-population.

9. "Audio Today," and "State of the News," as cited in "Radio Facts and Figures."

10. "Weekly Time Spent Listening to The Radio in the United States as of June 2016, by Age and Gender," *Statista*, accessed October, 2016, https://www.statista.com/statistics/252204/weekly-time-spent-listening-to-the-radio-in-the-us-by-age-and-gender

11. "Number of Facebook Users in the United States from 2015 to 2021," *Statista*, accessed March 11, 2017, https://www.statista.com/statistics/408971/number-of-us-facebook-users

12. "Audio Today," and "State of the News," as cited in "Radio Facts and Figures."

13. "Top Tens: Prime Broadcast Network TV – United States," *Nielsen*, accessed October, 2016, http://www.nielsen.com/us/en/top10s.html

14. "Nielsen Estimates 116.4 Million TV Homes in the U.S. for the 2015-16 TV Season," *Nielsen*, August 28, 2015, http://www.nielsen.com/us/en/insights/news/2015/nielsen-estimates-116-4-million-tv-homes-in-the-us-for-the-2015-16-tv-season.html

15. "Audio Today," and "State of the News," as cited in "Radio Facts and Figures."

16. "The State of Traditional TV: Updated with Q3 2016 Data," *Marketing Charts*, January 11, 2017, http://www.marketingcharts.com/television/are-young-people-watching-less-tv-24817

17. John Koblin, "How Much Do We Love TV? Let Us Count the Ways," *The New York Times*, June 30, 2016, https://www.nytimes.com/2016/07/01/business/media/nielsen-survey-media-viewing.html

18. "Consumers Notice Roadside Posters More than Digital Media," *Outdoor Advertising Association of America*, March 6, 2017, http://oaaa.org/StayConnected/PressReleases/tabid/327/id/4840/Default.aspx

19. Based on population data and information from "Internet Usage in the United States - Statistics & Facts," *Statista*, accessed March 12, 2017, https://www.statista.com/topics/2237/internet-usage-in-the-united-states

20. Roxanne Bauer, "Media (R)evolutions: Time Spend Online Continues to Rise," *The World Bank*, February 10, 2016, http://blogs.worldbank.org/publicsphere/media-revolutions-time-spent-online-continues-rise

21. Evan Asano, "How Much Time Do People Spend on Social Media?," *Social Media Today*, January 4, 2017, http://www.socialmediatoday.com/marketing/how-much-time-do-people-spend-social-media-infographic

22. "Percentage of U.S. Population with a Social Media Profile 2008-2017," *Statista*, accessed March 11, 2017, https://www.statista.com/statistics/273476/percentageof-us-population-with-a-social-network-profile

23. Erik Devaney, "Why Don't My Facebook Fans See My Posts? The Decline of Organic Facebook Reach," *HubSpot*, April 7, 2016, https://blog.hubspot.com/marketing/facebook-declining-organic-reach

24. There are some strict rules around SMS marketing and how to invite customers to opt-in. You'll want to look into the rules surrounding this before setting up this kind of marketing.

25. "Year in Review 2016," *Campaign Monitor*, accessed March 12, 2017, https://www.campaignmonitor.com/company/annual-report/2016

26. There are strict rules around how you can communicate with your customers via email. If you decide to publish an e-newsletter, make sure you are up to date on the rules and guidelines before you start.

27. Paul Gillin, "RIP Pittsburgh Tribune-Review," *Newspaper Death Watch*, September 28, 2016, http://www.newspaperdeathwatch.com

28. "Postmedia Reports Fourth Quarter Results," *Postmedia*, October 20, 2016, http://www.postmedia.com/2016/10/20/postmedia-reports-fourth-quarter-results-2

29. Michael Barthel, "Newspapers: Fact Sheet," *Pew Research Center*, last updated June 2016, http://www.journalism.org/2016/06/15/newspapers-fact-sheet

30. "Average Number of Readers of Any Daily Newspaper (Print Edition) Per Issue in the United States from Spring 2008 to Spring 2016," *Statista*, accessed March 12, 2017, https://www.statista.com/statistics/229535/readers-of-any-daily-newspaper-print-edition-per-issue

31. Rebecca Harris, "Why Printed Flyers Still Work," *Marketing*, December 1, 2015, http://www.marketingmag.ca/media/why-printed-flyers-still-work-162813

32. JobShop example and material contributed by Stacey Cattell.

CHAPTER 6

1. "Most Famous Social Network Sites Worldwide as of January 2017, Ranked by Number of Active Users," *Statista*, accessed March 12, 2017, https://www.statista.com/statistics/272014/global-social-networks-ranked-by-number-of-users

2. "Chart 26: Active Users of the Top Social Platforms and Messaging Tools, by Age," *GlobalWebIndex*, Q4, 2014, http://www.smartinsights.com/wp-content/uploads/2014/04/Demographic-use-of-social-networks-age-and-gender.jpg

3. Eva A. van Reijmersdal, "Mixing Advertising and Editorial Content in Radio Programs: Appreciation and Recall of Brand Placements Versus Commercials," *International Journal of Advertising* 30, no. 3 (2011).

4. Williams developed the "one dollar per person per year" guideline in response to the question "How do I know how many people I can afford to reach?" Although this answer is a simplification, it is a good starting point to give you an idea of the size of audience you can potentially brand yourself with this year. A full explanation of this guideline can be found in Roy H. Williams, "A Dollar a Person a Year," *The Monday Morning Memo*, July 1, 2002, http://www.mondaymorningmemo.com/newsletters/a-dollar-a-person-a-year

Chapter 7

1. Sample survey material in this chapter contributed by Lang McGilp of Insightrix Research.

BIBLIOGRAPHY

"5 Things You Never Knew About Santa Claus and Coca-Cola." *Coca-Cola Journey*. January 1, 2012. http://www.coca-colacompany.com/stories/coke-lore-santa-claus.

"75 Customer Service Facts, Quotes and Statistics: How Your Business Can Deliver with the Best of the Best." *Help Scout*. Accessed January, 2017. https://www.helpscout.net/75-customer-service-facts-quotes-statistics.

AJ. "10 of the Highest Paid Celebrity Endorsement Deals." *The Richest*. February 2, 2015. http://www.therichest.com/expensive-lifestyle/money/10-of-the-highest-paid-celebrity-endorsement-deals.

"AM/FM Reach is High; Time-Spent Is Nuanced." *RAIN News*. June 27, 2016. http://rainnews.com/amfm-reach-is-high-time-spent-is-nuanced-nielsen-report.

"Annual Radio Revenue Trends." *Radio Advertising Bureau*. Accessed October, 2016. http://www.rab.com/public/pr/rev-pr.cfm.

Asano, Evan. "How Much Time Do People Spend on Social Media?" *Social Media Today*. January 4, 2017. http://www.socialmediatoday.com/marketing/how-much-time-do-people-spend-social-media-infographic.

"Audio Today: Radio 2016 – Appealing Far and Wide." *Nielsen*. February 25, 2016. http://www.nielsen.com/us/en/insights/reports/2016/audio-today-radio-2016-appealing-far-and-wide.html.

"Average Number of Readers of Any Daily Newspaper (Print Edition) Per Issue in the United States from Spring 2008 to Spring 2016." *Statista.* Accessed March 12, 2017. https://www.statista.com/statistics/229535/readers-of-any-daily-newspaper-print-edition-per-issue.

Barthel, Michael. "Newspapers: Fact Sheet." *Pew Research Center.* Last updated June 2016. http://www.journalism.org/2016/06/15/newspapers-fact-sheet.

Bauer, Roxanne. "Media (R)evolutions: Time Spend Online Continues to Rise." *The World Bank.* February 10, 2016. http://blogs.worldbank.org/publicsphere/media-revolutions-time-spent-online-continues-rise.

Bellman, Sarah. "15 Most Iconic Celebrity Endorsements." *Who Say.* September 29, 2014. http://www.whosay.com/articles/4317-15-most-iconic-celebrity-endorsements.

Bennett, Shea. "How Many Millennials, Gen Xers and Baby Boomers Use Facebook, Twitter, and Instagram?." *Adweek.* June 3, 2014. http://www.adweek.com/socialtimes/millennials-gen-x-baby-boomers-social-media/499110.

Bradshaw, James. "Yellow Pages to Re-evaluate Demand for Home Delivery of Directory." *The Globe and Mail.* Last updated February 2, 2015. http://www.theglobeandmail.com/report-on-business/yellow-pages-to-re-evaluate-demand-for-home-delivery-of-its-directory/article22753414.

"Brand Communities and Consumer Tribes." *Vivid Brand.* Accessed September, 2016. http://vividbrand.com/views/brand-communities-and-consumer-tribes.

Brecht, Robert M. "Do Celebrity Endorsements Equal Advertising Effectiveness?" *DMN3.* May 8, 2012. https://www.dmn3.com/dmn3-blog/do-celebrity-endorsements-equal-advertising-effectiveness.

"Building a Tribe: How to Create a Following for Your Brand." *Wasp Buzz*. November 17, 2010. http://www.waspbarcode.com/buzz/building-a-tribe-how-to-create-a-following-for-your-brand.

Canada Post. *Direct Mail and Digital Media: An Integrated One-to-One Marketing that Drives Results*. August 2010. https://www.canadapost.ca/cpo/mc/assets/pdf/business/dm_dm_en.pdf

Chaffey, Dave. "Global Social Media Research Summary 2017." *Smart Insights*. February 27, 2017. http://www.smartinsights.com/social-media-marketing/social-media-strategy/new-global-social-media-research.

"Chart 26: Active Users of the Top Social Platforms and Messaging Tools, by Age." *GlobalWebIndex*. Q4, 2014. http://www.smartinsights.com/wp-content/uploads/2014/04/Demographic-use-of-social-networks-age-and-gender.jpg.

Clay, Felix. "7 Shockingly Bad Slogans Major Corporations Went With." *Cracked*. January 29, 2015. http://www.cracked.com/blog/the-7-worst-slogans-in-history-advertising.

"Consumers Notice Roadside Posters More than Digital Media." *Outdoor Advertising Association of America*. March 6, 2017. http://oaaa.org/StayConnected/PressReleases/tabid/327/id/4840/Default.aspx.

Dan, Avi. "The Real Reason that Super Bowl Ads Are Worth the Money." *Forbes*. January 28, 2013. http://www.forbes.com/sites/avidan/2013/01/28/the-real-reason-that-super-bowl-ads-are-worth-the-money.

Devaney, Erik. "Why Don't My Facebook Fans See My Posts? The Decline of Organic Facebook Reach." *HubSpot*. April 7, 2016. https://blog.hubspot.com/marketing/facebook-declining-organic-reach.

"Direct Mail Data Spending in the United States from 2010 to 2016."
Statista. Accessed March 12, 2017. https://www.statista.com/
statistics/466501/direct-mail-data-spend-usa.

Dudler, Roger. "14 of the Happiest Brands of All Time." *Frontify*.
Accessed October, 2016. https://frontify.com/blog/14-of-the-
happiest-brands-of-all-time.

Furgison, Lisa. "The Ultimate Guide to 'Google My Business'."
Vertical Response. October 15, 2015. http://www.verticalresponse.
com/blog/the-ultimate-guide-to-google-my-business.

Gillin, Paul. "RIP Pittsburgh Tribune-Review." *Newspaper Death
Watch*. September 28, 2016. http://www.newspaperdeathwatch.
com.

Hangen, Nathan. "David Ogilvy's 7 Tips for Writing Copy that Sells."
Kissmetrics. Accessed October, 2016. https://blog.kissmetrics.
com/david-ogilvy.

Harris, Rebecca. "Why Printed Flyers Still Work." *Marketing*.
December 1, 2015. http://www.marketingmag.ca/media/why-
printed-flyers-still-work-162813.

Hepburn, Matthew. "The Share a Coke Story." *Coca-Cola Journey*.
Accessed September, 2016. http://www.coca-cola.co.uk/stories/
share-a-coke.

"Internet Usage in the United States - Statistics & Facts." *Statista*.
Accessed March 12, 2017. https://www.statista.com/
topics/2237/internet-usage-in-the-united-states.

Johnson, Lauren. "IAB Study Says 26% of Desktop Users Turn On
Ad Blockers." *Adweek*. July 26, 2016. http://www.adweek.com/
news/technology/iab-study-says-26-desktop-users-turn-ad-
blockers-172665.

Koblin, John. "How Much Do We Love TV? Let Us Count the Ways." *The New York Times*. June 30, 2016. https://www.nytimes.com/2016/07/01/business/media/nielsen-survey-media-viewing.html.

Koch, Wendy. "Phone-book Delivery Disappearing." *USA Today*. Last updated June 2, 2011. http://usatoday30.usatoday.com/news/nation/environment/2011-06-01-phone-books-disappearing_n.htm.

Kuzma, Tom. "Why You Should Be Using Video Marketing Now!" *5 Tales*. August 17, 2016. https://www.5tales.com.au/blog/video-marketing.

Marcucci, Carl. "The Power of Radio Personalities." *Radio and Television Business Report*. April 14, 2014. http://rbr.com/the-power-of-radio-personalities.

Mints, Lauren. "How to Determine the Perfect Marketing Budget for Your Company." *Entrepreneur*. March 11, 2015. https://www.entrepreneur.com/article/243790.

"Most Famous Social Network Sites Worldwide as of January 2017, Ranked by Number of Active Users." *Statista*. Accessed March 12, 2017. https://www.statista.com/statistics/272014/global-social-networks-ranked-by-number-of-users.

"Negative Reviews: A Golden Opportunity for Business." *Better Business Bureau*. September 15, 2014. https://www.bbb.org/phoenix/news-events/business-tips/2014/09/negative-reviews-a-golden-opportunity-for-business.

Nicholas, Jimmy. *Small Business Marketing: Your Ultimate Guide*. Waterford, CT: JE2000, 2013.

"Nielsen Estimates 116.4 Million TV Homes in the U.S. for the 2015-16 TV Season." *Nielsen*. August 28, 2015. http://www.nielsen.com/us/en/insights/news/2015/nielsen-estimates-116-4-million-tv-homes-in-the-us-for-the-2015-16-tv-season.html.

Nowak, Peter. "The Skeptics Said Streaming Music Would Kill Satellite Radio. They Were Wrong." *Canadian Business*. April 7, 2016. http://www.canadianbusiness.com/innovation/the-skeptics-said-streaming-music-would-kill-satellite-radio-they-were-wrong.

"Number of Facebook Users in the United States from 2015 to 2021." *Statista*. Accessed March 11, 2017. https://www.statista.com/statistics/408971/number-of-us-facebook-users.

"Oreo's Super Bowl Tweet: 'You Can Still Dunk in The Dark'." *Huffington Post*. Last updated April 6, 2013. http://www.huffingtonpost.com/2013/02/04/oreos-super-bowl-tweet-dunk-dark_n_2615333.html.

"Percentage of U.S. Population with a Social Media Profile 2008-2017." *Statista*. Accessed March 11, 2017. https://www.statista.com/statistics/273476/percentage-of-us-population-with-a-social-network-profile.

"Postmedia Reports Fourth Quarter Results." *Postmedia*. October 20, 2016. http://www.postmedia.com/2016/10/20/postmedia-reports-fourth-quarter-results-2.

"Radio Facts and Figures." *News Generation*. Accessed October, 2016. http://www.newsgeneration.com/broadcast-resources/radio-facts-and-figures.

"Radio: The Online Multiplier." *Radiocentre*. Accessed April 23, 2017. http://www.radiocentre.org/studies/radio-the-online-multiplier/

Randolph, James. "How to Use the Social Media Rule of Thirds." *Change Conversations*. November 11, 2016. https://www.marketing-partners.com/conversations2/how-to-use-the-social-media-rule-of-thirds.

Read, Ash. "Facebook Organic Reach is Dying: Here's Why It's a Good Thing." *Unbounce*. October 3, 2016. http://unbounce.com/social-media/facebook-organic-reach-is-dying-heres-why-its-a-good-thing.

Ritson, Mark. *Ritson vs Social Media*. Video, 34:27. January 7, 2015. https://www.youtube.com/watch?v=S2NUayn2vP0.

Sass, Eric. "Half of U.S. Listeners Tune into Online Radio." *Media Daily News*. March 5, 2014. http://www.mediapost.com/publications/article/220860/half-of-us-listeners-tune-into-online-radio.html.

Schaal, Dennis. "Travel Booking Sites Spent $624 Million on TV Advertising in 2014." *Skift*. December 31, 2014. https://skift.com/2014/12/31/booking-sites-spent-624-million-on-tv-advertising-in-2014-expedia-dominated.

Schultz, Howard. Pour Your Heart into It: How Starbucks Built a Company One Cup at a Time. New York: Hyperion, 1997.

Shapley, Dan. "In San Francisco, Phone Books Will Be Optional." *The Daily Green.* May 18, 2011. http://preview.www.thedailygreen.com/environmental-news/latest/san-francisco-phone-book-ban.

Sinek, Simon. *Start with Why: How Great Leaders Inspire Everyone to Take Action*. New York: Penguin, 2009.

Slywotsky, Adrian. *The Art of Profitability.* New York: Hachette, 2002.

"Social Media's Massive Failure." *The Ad Contrarian*. March 21, 2011. http://adcontrarian.blogspot.ca/2011/03/social-medias-massive-failure.html.

"State of the News Media 2015." *Pew Research Center*. April 2015. http://www.journalism.org/files/2015/04/final-state-of-the-news-media1.pdf.

Suggett, Paul. "The 100 Best Advertising Taglines Ever." *The Balance*. Last updated February 3, 2017. https://www.thebalance.com/best-advertising-taglines-ever-39208.

"Tagline Hall of Shame." *Tagline Guru*. Accessed February 6, 2017. http://www.taglineguru.com/tagline_hall_of_shame.html.

Terlep, Sharon and Deepa Seetharaman. "P&G to Scale Back Targeted Facebook Ads." *The Wall Street Journal*. August 17, 2016. http://www.wsj.com/articles/p-g-to-scale-back-targeted-facebook-ads-1470760949.

"The 25 Worst Advertising Slogans of All Time." *World Wide Interweb*. December 2, 2016. http://worldwideinterweb.com/10663-worst-advertising-slogans-of-all-time-gallery.

"The Global Standard for Measuring Radio Advertising Effectiveness." *Canadian Broadcast Sales*. Accessed April 24, 2017. http://www.radiocbs.com/showpage.php?pageid=19

"The Nielsen Total Audience Report: Q1 2016." *Neilsen*. June 27, 2016. http://www.nielsen.com/us/en/insights/reports/2016/the-total-audience-report-q1-2016.html.

"The State of Traditional TV: Updated with Q3 2016 Data." *Marketing Charts*. January 11, 2017. http://www.marketingcharts.com/television/are-young-people-watching-less-tv-24817.

Thiel, Peter. *Zero to One: Notes on Startups, or How to Build the Future*. New York: Crown Publishing, 2014.

"Top Tens: Prime Broadcast Network TV – United States." *Nielsen*. Accessed October, 2016. http://www.nielsen.com/us/en/top10s.html.

Topper, Steve. "Are You Advertising to a Moving Parade or a Standing Army?" *Deluxe*. August 31, 2010. http://fi.deluxe. com/community-blog/financial-marketing-insights/are-you-advertising-to-a-moving-parade-or-a-standing-army.

"US Online and Traditional Media Advertising Outlook, 2016-2020." *Marketing Charts*. June 14, 2016. http://www.marketingcharts. com/traditional/us-online-and-traditional-media-advertising-outlook-2016-2020-68214.

"US Population." *WorldoMeters*. Accessed March 12, 2017. http:// www.worldometers.info/world-population/us-population.

van Reijmersdal, Eva A. "Mixing Advertising and Editorial Content in Radio Programs: Appreciation and Recall of Brand Placements Versus Commercials." *International Journal of Advertising* 30, no. 3 (2011).

Virgillito, Dan. "Which Social Media Platforms Offer the Greatest Organic Reach?" *Elegant Themes*. January 7, 2016. https:// www.elegantthemes.com/blog/resources/which-social-media-platforms-offer-the-greatest-organic-reach.

Waxman, Martin. *Social Media Marketing for Small Business*. Online course, 59:22. August 16, 2016. https://www.linkedin.com/learning/social-media-marketing-for-small-business.

"Weekly Time Spent Listening to the Radio in the United States as of June 2016, by Age and Gender." *Statista*. Accessed October, 2016. https://www.statista.com/statistics/252204/weekly-time-spent-listening-to-the-radio-in-the-us-by-age-and-gender.

White, Abigail. "Organic Reach on Instagram Is Dead, Brands Scurry to Figure Out the New Algorithm." *The American Genius*. March 28, 2016. https://theamericangenius.com/social-media/organic-reach-instagram-dead.

Williams, Roy H. "A Dollar a Person a Year." *The Monday Morning Memo*. July 1, 2002. http://www.mondaymorningmemo.com/newsletters/a-dollar-a-person-a-year.

—. *Secret Formulas of the Wizard of Ads*. Austin, TX: Bard Press, 1999.

—. "So You Want to Be a Writer." *The Monday Morning Memo*. June 2, 2003. http://www.mondaymorningmemo.com/newsletters/so-you-want-to-be-a-writer.

—. "The Future of Advertising." *The Monday Morning Memo*. May 24, 2004. http://www.mondaymorningmemo.com/newsletters/the-future-of-advertising.

—. "The New Language of Effective Ads." *The Monday Morning Memo*. November 8, 2008. http://www.mondaymorningmemo.com/newsletters/the-new-language-of-effective-ads.

"Year in Review 2016." *Campaign Monitor*. Accessed March 12, 2017. https://www.campaignmonitor.com/company/annual-report/2016.

Young Entrepreneur Council. "10 Tips for a Remarkable Tagline." *Inc.* July 19, 2013. http://www.inc.com/young-entrepreneur-council/10-tips-for-a-remarkable-tagline.html.

About the Author

Daria Malin is the founder of Boost Strategic Coaching. She works with business owners and professionals to establish proper practices in business development, becoming a trusted source of support, guidance, and accountability. Daria is a sought after speaker and trainer on marketing, sales, advertising, and professional reputation and leadership.

Daria built her career in media advertising sales where she was instrumental in the success of hundreds of marketing campaigns and promotions. She has a Bachelor of Commerce degree from the University of Saskatchewan, and is a graduate of The Wizard Academy Nontraditional Business School in Austin, Texas taught by Roy H. Williams, founder of the Academy and author of the bestselling *Wizard of Ads* book series.

To book Daria to speak at your conference or event, please email: info@boostcoaching.ca.

ABOUT BOOST STRATEGIC COACHING

Boost Strategic Coaching is a business coaching firm that works with experienced business owners and sales professionals to line up their branding, sales, and marketing. The goal is to get your business firing on all cylinders and further business development while avoiding costly mistakes of investing in marketing activities that don't work. We choose our clients as carefully as they choose us.

Too often, good business owners and professionals miss the mark because of how they communicate with their audience during business development. We know that "throwing a bunch of stuff at the wall and seeing what sticks" is not the way you want to run your sales and marketing. We guide clients through clear strategy and tactical implementation to ensure you get a maximum return on your efforts. We also give you the tools you need to create a system and execute a plan with purpose. We're here to help you hit your target.

Boost Strategic Coaching
www.boostcoaching.ca

Made in the
USA
Middletown, DE